Kneale's Guide To The Isle Of Man

W. Kneale.

DOUGLAS ISLE OF MAN

Douglas, Isle of Man

KNEALE'S GUIDE

TO THE

ISLE OF MAN,

COMPRISING

AN ACCOUNT OF THE ISLAND,

Historical, Physical, Archæological, & Topographical,

AND ALL THE INFORMATION DESIRABLE

FOR VISITORS AND TOURISTS.

TO WHICH IS APPENDED

𝕬 𝕮𝖔𝖑𝖑𝖊𝖈𝖙𝖎𝖔𝖓 𝖔𝖋 𝕰𝖓𝖙𝖊𝖗𝖙𝖆𝖎𝖓𝖎𝖓𝖌 𝕸𝖆𝖓𝖝 𝕷𝖊𝖌𝖊𝖓𝖉𝖘.

ILLUSTRATED WITH NUMEROUS ENGRAVINGS.

LONDON: G. PHILIP & SON, 32, FLEET STREET;
DOUGLAS: W. KNEALE, 37, DUKE STREET.

[ENTERED AT STATIONERS' HALL.]

PREFACE.

THE Guide-book now offered to the public, I believe, will more fully meet the requirements of visitors and tourists than any previous work of this description. It contains much curious and interesting information not to be found even in the most copious histories and descriptions of the Isle of Man.

Restricted by the limits of this little book, the writer has been compelled to be very brief in his statements. In drawing up chapters II. and III., which incorporate the latest results of historical investigation, he has consulted all the principal authorities: he has, moreover, given a large amount of information from his own researches. Considerable space in this volume is devoted to the antiquities of the isle. Several old crosses and other relics of the past, hitherto unnoticed, are here briefly described. The engravings of ancient crosses in the following pages are copied from the admirable etchings of Mr. W. Kinnebrook, published in 1841; and from representations given in Professor Worsaae's Account of the Danes and Northmen.

In this Guide-book will be found a list of the principal and most agreeable places of resort in the Isle of Man, which presents innumerable attractions to the lover of sublime and romantic scenery. Copious itineraries of routes are given, and the tourist is supplied with full information concerning hotels, distances, and conveyances.

A separate chapter, not the least entertaining in the book, is devoted to the legends of the isle.

Two photographs, which adorn the best edition of this work, call for a word of passing notice, both on account of the eminence of the personages represented in them, and the artistic skill displayed in their production. These beautiful portraits of an ancient king and queen of Man (William de Montagu, second Earl of Salisbury, and his Countess) were executed from elaborate drawings made by a lineal descendant of the above-mentioned king, for G. H. Wood, Esq. I am indebted to that gentleman for permission to copy these remarkable portraits, and for the use he has afforded me of many interesting MSS. relating to Manx history.

For much valuable information contained in these pages the sincere thanks of the writer are due to Laurence Adamson, Esq., Seneschal of the Isle of Man; and to C. N. Warton, Esq., of Lincoln's Inn, Barrister-at-Law.

W. K.

CONTENTS.

LIST OF ILLUSTRATIONS

IN THE SHILLING EDITION.*

* *A large map and numerous steel engravings will be found in the more expensive editions of this work.*

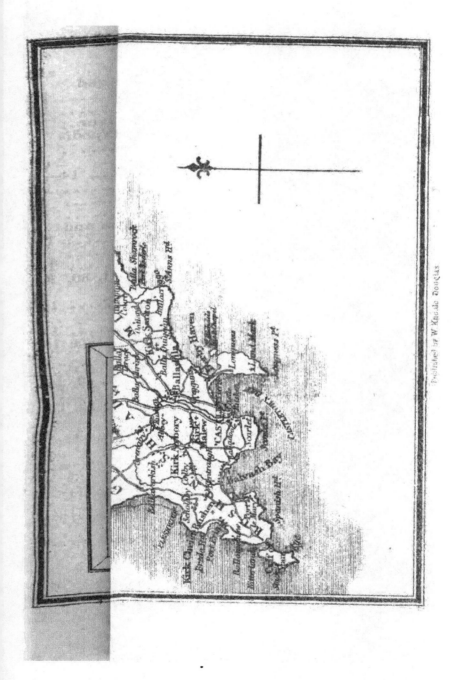

Publishel by W Kneale Douglas

KNEALE'S

GUIDE TO THE ISLE OF MAN.

———◦◇◦———

CHAPTER I.

GENERAL DESCRIPTION—CLIMATE—POPULATION—LAN-
GUAGE—REVENUE—COMMERCE, ETC.

> "Elysian island of the west,
> Still be thy gardens brighten'd by the rose
> Of a perennial spring, and winter's snows
> Ne'er chill the warmth of thy parental breast!
>
>   *   *   *   *   *
>
> Thou gem, half claim'd by earth, and half by sea,
> May blessings, like a flood, thy homes o'erflow,
> And health, though elsewhere lost, be found in thee!
> May thy bland zephyrs to the pallid cheek
> Of sickness ever roseate hues restore,
> And they who shun the rabble and the roar
> Of the wide world, on thy delightful shore
> Obtain that soft seclusion which they seek!"
>
> D. M. MOIR.

> "For sure so fair a place was never seen
>   Of all that ever charmed romantic eye:
> It seemed an emerald in the silver sheen
>   Of the bright waters; or, as when on high,
> Through clouds of fleecy white, laughs the cerulean sky."
>
> KEATS.

ALL the world knows, or ought to know, that in any
enumeration of the watering-places of the kingdom,
the Isle of Man must undoubtedly hold a distinguished place. This far-famed isle is situated in St.

George's Channel, and is nearly equidistant from
Ulster, Galloway, and Cumberland. Accessible by
its position, abounding in historical associations,
celebrated for its salubrious climate, its pellucid
waters, its natural phenomena—which offer a rich
field of exploration to the scientific traveller,—its
Keltic and Scandinavian antiquities, its noble range
of mountains, its romantic rural prospects, and for
the wild magnificence of its coast scenery, it cannot
be thought surprising that this "gem of the sea"
should attract the attention of countless hosts of
British tourists. In consequence of the cheapness
and facility of communication between England and
the miniature realm of Man, produced by the splendid
steamers of the Insular Packet Company, myriads of
pleasure-seekers are annually induced to visit this
enchanting isle, of which we proceed to offer a con-
cise, but comprehensive and accurate account.

Viewed from a distance, the Isle of Man—

"Whose rocky shore beats back the envious siege
Of watery Neptune"—

presents the appearance of "a dark cloud hanging
over the boundary of the waters, or, as an old
writer says, it looks like ane parke in ye seae im-
paled with rocks. As the voyager approaches this
little territory, the altitude of its mountains seems to
rise before him. Down their sloping sides, rocks and
ravines meet his view, whilst, in passing along the
shore, the glens and bases of the hills present many
objects of rural beauty and scenes of romantic
grandeur." The shores of this charming isle are
girded by bold, rugged, and precipitous cliffs, and
indented with capacious harbours and innumerable
creeks. In its greatest length the Isle of Man is
about thirty-three, in its greatest breadth about
thirteen miles. Its circumference is about seventy-
five miles, excluding the sinuosities of the bays;
and it contains a superficial area of about one

hundred and thirty thousand acres, or two hundred and three square miles. Its centre is in latitude 54° 16′ north, and longitude 4° 30′ west. A chain of mountains traverses the isle from south-west to north-east. The following is a tabular list of the principal heights:—

Snaefell	2024	feet.
North Barrull (pronounced Barrool)	1842	,,
Slieau Choar	1797	,,
Beinn-y-Phot (pronounced Penny-pot)	1772	,,
Slieau-ny-Fraughane	1598	,,
Colden	1591	,,
South Barrull (Wardfell)	1584	,,
Sartfell	1560	,,
Slieau Chiarn	1533	,,
Garraghan	1520	,,
Cairn Garjohl	1449	,,
Cronk-ny-Irey-Lhaa	1445	,,
Greeba (southern summit)	1373	,,
Slieau Doo	1139	,,
Slieau Whuaillan (or Aalin)	1086	,,

The prospect from the summit of Snaefell is unspeakably grand—the ranges of Snowdon and Cumberland being visible to the southward and eastward; the mountains of Morne and Fairhead in Ireland appearing on the west side, and the Mull of Galloway, with the elevation of Criffell, rising in the northern horizon. A magnificent and inexpressibly beautiful view of the island, decked with a thousand charms, is also obtainable from this elevated spot.

> "Thou who would'st see the lovely and the wild
> Mingled in harmony on nature's face,
> Ascend our rocky mountains. Let thy foot
> Fail not with weariness, for on their tops
> The beauty and the majesty of earth,
> Spread wide beneath, shall make thee to forget
> The steep and toilsome way. There, as thou stand'st,
> The haunts of men below thee, and around
> The mountain summits, thy expanding heart
> Shall feel a kindred with that loftier world
> To which thou art translated, and partake
> The enlargement of thy vision."

A 2

Enjoying the benefit of the Gulf Stream, that
"great thermal ocean-river, incessantly flowing from
warmer to colder regions, diffusing warmth and
moisture along its course," the climate of the isle is
singularly mild and genial, and, being extremely
equable, is conducive to health and longevity. The
following data are the result of observations as published in the Registrar-General's Reports, taking an
average of seven years, ending September, 1860 :—
Summer (June, July, and August), mean temperature,
56°·17; Autumn (September, October, and November), mean temperature, 46°·97 ; Winter (December,
January, February), mean temperature, 40°·90;
Spring (March, April, May), mean temperature,
44°·70; mean annual rain-fall, 30·2 inches. According to the Reports of the English and Scottish
Meteorological Societies, the mean annual temperature is 47°·8. The vigorous health of the inhabitants
attests the extreme salubrity of the climate.

. The Isle of Man possesses almost every variety of
natural charm—the fertile and richly cultivated
plain, the secluded valley, the majestic mountain, the
river, "winding at its own sweet will," and the picturesque cascade. To the admirer of nature it
presents indeed a rare combination of attractions:—

"A blending of all beauties; streams and dells,
  Fruit, foliage, crag, wood, cornfield, mountain, vine;
  And chiefless castles, breathing stern farewells,
  From grey but leafy walls where ruin greenly dwells."

The isle has few rivers with a large volume of
water. The principal one rises by numerous branches
from the declivities which surround Snaefell, and,
passing in a tortuous course by Sulby, is discharged
into the sea at Ramsey. The Doo and the Glass,
whose sources are on the mountains of Marown and
Braddan, unite, and fall into the sea at Douglas.
The Silverburn, which rises on South Barrull, dis-
charges its waters into Castletown Bay. Laxey river

has its sources around Snaefell. The Neb, which takes its rise in the mountains of Michael, flows into the sea at Peel. There are many beautiful cascades in the island, amongst which may be enumerated Spooyt Vane in Michael, and those at Glen Meay, Glen Helen (Rhennass), Ballaglass, and Hamilton Bridge.

Douglas, Ramsey, Castletown, and Peel, are the towns; and Ballasalla, Laxey, Port St. Mary, Derbyhaven, Port Erin, Michael, and Ballaugh, the principal villages. Castletown is the capital of the isle.

Prior to the revestment of the sovereignty in the British crown in the year 1765, agriculture appears to have been greatly neglected, the exertions of the peasantry being devoted to the herring fishery and the contraband trade. Since that period, however, great improvements have taken place. The soil, though varying in its nature and quality, is, when properly cultivated, capable of producing crops not inferior to those raised in England. Scattered through the isle are farmers of British origin, who have gradually introduced the most improved methods of cultivating their lands. For the information of agriculturists, we subjoin a statement of the succession of crops:—first year, oats; second year, root crop; third year, wheat, barley, or oats, seeded down and kept in grass from one to three years, when it is generally broken up with oats, but sometimes with wheat.

According to the last census (1861), the population of the isle amounts to 52,252. In 1851, it was 52,387; in 1841, 47,975; in 1831, 41,000; in 1821, 40,081; in 1784, 24,924; in 1757, 19,144; in 1726, 14,070. At the beginning of the eighth century, according to the venerable Bede, it consisted of about three hundred families. "An old rhyme," says the *Liverpool Mercury*, "recommends that spinsters should be sent to the Isle of Man, and bachelors to the Scilly Isles.

With respect to the latter recommendation, it will be
prudent not to offer an opinion, but as to the former
it will be well to guard our fair marriageable friends
from entertaining the idea that in the Isle of Man
there is a superabundant stock of the genus *homo*.
The fact is that according to the last census there is
in a population of 52,252 an excess of 3336 females,
1621 of that excess being in the town of Douglas
alone." The Manx are generally tall, robust, frank,
hospitable, enterprising, and intelligent. Few of the
natives have attained any distinguished literary,
scientific, or political eminence. This isle, however,
has produced some celebrated individuals. Among
the most notable are the late Rev. Dr. Kelly, author
of a dictionary and grammar of the Manx language ;
the late Rev. Dr. Stowell, president of Cheshunt
College, editor of the *Eclectic Review*, and author of
several theological treatises; the late Professor Forbes,
of the university of Edinburgh, whose name "will go
down to posterity inseparably linked with the history
of palæontology, as one of the greatest naturalists
that ever strove to bring his knowledge of the living
world to elucidate the physical and organic changes
in the past history of the earth;" the late Miss
Nelson, authoress of a volume of poems entitled
"Island Minstrelsy;" the late Colonel Wilkes,
governor of St. Helena when Napoleon Buonaparte
was a prisoner on that isle; the late Sir Mark Cubbon,
chief commissioner of Mysore, in India; G. H.
Wood, Esq., author of two volumes of poems (to one
of which are appended metaphysical critiques), and of
various religious and philosophical publications; the
Rev. Dr. Lyons; the Rev. Canon Stowell, M.A., of
Manchester; the Rev. Hugh Stowell Brown, of
Liverpool; and the Rev. T. E. Brown, M.A., one of
the contributors to Dr. W. Smith's elaborate and
invaluable "Dictionary of the Bible."

The Manx language is one of the six dialects of

the Keltic. Philologists have shown that the Keltic tongues, which are divided into high and low (the high being the Welsh, Cornish, and Armorican—the low being the Erse division, or the Gaelic, Irish, and Manx), belong to the class of Indo-European languages. Of these six Keltic dialects, the Irish and the Gaelic most nearly approximate. Of the three languages which constitute the Erse division, the Gaelic is supposed by some to have the highest pretentions to antiquity. Mr. Garnett, however, one of the most learned of English philologists, maintains "that Irish is the parent tongue, that Scottish Gaelic is Irish stripped of a few inflexions, and that Manx is merely Gaelic with a few peculiar words, and disguised by a corrupt system of orthography." It is worthy of remark that the phonetic system of orthography has been adopted by Manx scholars, who are fond of expatiating upon the harmony and melody of the Manx, which, they assert, is a noble, copious, dignified, and sonorous tongue. In it are discoverable indelible traces of the Icelandic or Old Norse language—the language of the Scandinavian conquerors of Man. At the beginning of the nineteenth century, the Manx tongue was generally understood through the Isle of Man, and was used in the Church services of many of the districts remote from the principal towns. Now, however, it is rarely used in conversation, except among the peasantry, and a Manx sermon is seldom heard; "and though the language is still employed in some official formulæ of the Tynwald (or ancient court)—in the same manner as, in our parliamentary proceedings, *la Reine le veult* is still the Norman form in which the royal assent is given to an act of parliament —the ancient idiom of Mona is very near extinction." A grammar and a dictionary were composed, nearly a century ago, by the Rev. Dr. Kelly. In 1835 a dictionary was compiled by Archibald Cregeen, who

remarks that the Manx tongue "appears like a piece
of exquisite net-work, interwoven together in a
masterly manner, and framed by the hands of a most
skilful workman. The depth of meaning that
abounds in many of the words must be conspicuous
to every person versed in the language." The native
literature consists of a legendary ballad, composed in
1520, narrating the fortunes of the various possessors
of the isle; the ballad concerning Illiam Dhone; the
ballad of Molley Charane; political and satirical
poems and songs; carvals or carols; translations of
the Bible, of the Book of Common Prayer, of portions of Milton's "Paradise Lost,"* of "The
Hermit," by Parnell, of Cowper's "Verses supposed
to be written by Alexander Selkirk," of Doddridge's
"Rise and Progress of Religion in the Soul," of
hymns by Wesley, Watts, and others; of various
religious tracts, and of several theological works by
the celebrated Bishop Wilson. As specimens of the
language, we subjoin the Lord's Prayer, and a few
proverbial sayings, &c., with interlinear English
versions :—

Ayr   ain   t'ayns niau, Casheric dy row dt' ennym.
Father our who art in heaven, Holy (may) be thy name.
Dy jig dty reeriaght.   Dt' aigney dy row jeant er   y thalloo
Come thy kingdom. Thy will   be   done on the earth

---

* The Rev. Mr. Christian translated portions of Milton's
great epic into Manx verse. According to a well-known
Manx scholar, all the finest passages have been translated, and
all the "nonsense" has been suppressed. On my asking him
where the nonsense is to be found, he replied :—"'Teet, there's
a dale of nonsense in the English pome.. I mane the foolish
tales about Adam and Eve coortin', and such like. There's
none of that nonsense in the Manx pote-ry—no inteet. A dale
of Milton's 'Paradise Lost' is nauthin' in the world but
thrash. The Manx translation is far shoo-pay-re-er—pertick-
lerly those parts of the pome tellin' about the fights between
the divvels and the angels—yis, inteet. Aw, man, it's ray-ly
wun-thir-ful—it's grand—grand uncommon !"

myr te ayns niau.   Cur   dooin nyn arran   jiu   as   gagh
as it is in heaven.   Give to us our bread to-day and every
laa.   As   leih   dooin nyn loghtyn myr ta shin   leih
day.   And forgive to us our trespasses as are we forgive
dauesyn ta   jannoo   loghtyn nyn 'oi.   As   ny   leeid
to those are committing trespasses us against.   And not lead
shin ayns   miolagh ;   agh   livrey shin veih olk.   Son lhiats
us   into temptation; but deliver us from evil.   For thine
y   reeriaght,   as   y   phooar, as   y   ghloyr, son dy bragh
the kingdom, and the power, and the glory, for the ever
as   dy bragh.   Amen.
and the ever.   Amen.

" The Manx," says Robertson, " have the following
generous proverb :—

*Tra ta yn derrey Vought cooney lesh hought elley ta'see hene
garaghtee :* When one poor man relieves another, God himself
rejoices at it ; or, as it it is in the original, laughs outright."

Kecayl chionnit   yn   cheeayl share,
Wit   bought is the   wit   best,
Mannagh vel ee kionnit roo gheyr.
If it be   not bought too dear.

Caghlaa   obbyr   aaish.
Change of work is rest.

Easht   lesh   dagh cleaysh,   eisht jean briwnys.
Listen with each   ear,   then do judgment.

Ta ynsagh   coamrey   stoamrey yn dooinney berchagh ;   as te
Is learning the attire comely of the   man   rich; and it is
berchys   yn dooinney boght.
the riches of the   man   poor.

We shall conclude with one more specimen—a
translation of a passage from a celebrated philosopher
of antiquity :—

*Insh daue, cha nee shen ta'n aigney oc dy chlashtyn, agh shen nee
ad bwoishal dy beagh ad er chlashtyn ;—Lhig da choraa yn irriney
ne cheartyn roshtyn ny cleashyn shen ta dy kinjah geaishtagh rish,
as lhieent less brynneragh :* Dic illis non quod volunt audire, sed
quod audisse semper volent ;—Plenas aures adulationibus
aliquando vera vox intret.

SENECA DE BENEF. Lib 6. c. 33.

A return has recently been printed, by order of
the House of Commons, showing the total amount of

taxation levied in the Isle of Man, distinguishing
between direct and indirect taxation; of the sums
of money paid to the former lord and owners of the
island, for all rights, titles, property, or interest they
may have had or claimed to have had in the island,
and its surplus revenue for the last thirty years.
From this return it appears that the gross customs'
revenues for 1863, being indirect taxes, but taxes for
state purposes, amounted to £33,039 17s. 7d.   Under
tithe-rent charge the amount levied by the Tynwald
Act of 1839, in lieu of tithes subject to rise and fall
according to the price of corn, was £5,974; of this
amount there was £553 for state and £5,421 for local
purposes.   Referring to direct taxes, the same being
applied to local purposes, we find the following
items:—Highway rates, consisting of labour rate in
respect of lands, houses, and carts, estimated at
£2,678 10s.; assessed taxes (for support of the high-
ways and bridges) on spring carriages and dogs,
£1,028 10s.; licensed duties on hawkers, £20; on
public houses and private licenses, £1,215; game,
£102 10s.; bankers, £40; brewers, £30; advocates
(to the bar), £25; charge for paving, &c., the town
of Douglas, including 3s. per house to the highway
fund, levied by the town commissioners, amounted to
£1,760; paving the streets of Castletown, Peel, and
Ramsey, 6d. in the pound on the annual value of
property, £319 13s.; church-rate, average of £35 for
each parish, exclusive of extra rates for building
churches and providing new burial grounds, £595;
the Sumner's dues, estimated at £10 for each parish,
£170; parish clerks' dues, 1d. from every house-
holder, and 4d. for every plough in use, £92 13s. 4d.;
maintenance of poor, in lieu of poor rates, there
being church collections and various associations
established to receive contributions (the number of
paupers estimated about 500), collected annually
about £6,000.   There is a sum of £6,316 14s. 11d.

for land revenue of the Crown, ending 31st of March, 1863, and £75 for alienation fines, both of which are placed under the head of "direct taxes," but applicable for state purposes. The total amount of taxation for state purposes is £40,984 12s. 6d., and for local purposes, £19,497 6s. 4d., making an aggregate of £59,418 18s. 10d. We now come to an important and interesting branch of the returns, the sums paid to the former Lord of the Isle of Man for rights, &c. The first payment by the British Government was for customs duties, two castles, and other property, in the year 1765, the amount being £70,000; paid in 1826, for one-fourth of gross revenue, £150,000; for church patronage, quit rents, mines, demesne lands, and other property under sales to commissioners of the Treasury, dated respectively 13th March, 1826, 20th April, 1827, and 2nd June, 1828, the respective amounts of £100,000, £34,200, and £132,944, making a total of £487,144. Deducting a sum of £41,700 being £11,700 for property sold by the commissioners of the Treasury, and £30,000, value of crown commons, there remains a sum of £445,444 paid to the former Lord of the Isle for rights and privileges. In a report by the attorney and solicitor-generals of England in November, 1802, on certain claims then made by the Duke of Athol, they cite a portion of a report to the Treasury from the commissioners of customs and excise, which states that previous to the purchase of the Isle of Man the loss of revenue sustained by Great Britain alone amounted to £350,000 annually, or thereabouts. An increase, therefore, to the imperial revenue of not less than £350,000, which commenced from the year 1767, may be considered as one item of income from the purchase of the island. The total gross revenue (or thereabouts) derived from the island during the last 30 years, from 1833 to 1863, was £960,885 18s., and the total expenditure for the same period, £407,586 10s. 10d., leaving a surplus revenue for the period previously named of £553,299 7s. 2d. The revenue derived from the customs for the year ending March 31, 1864, was £33,978 1s. 11d.

The manufactures of the isle are inconsiderable: the principal are woollen cloths, linen, canvas, sail cloth, ropes, paper, soap, and starch. There are several iron foundries, ship-building yards, and water and gas companies. The list of exports comprehends corn, fish, horses, cattle, pigs, ropes, canvas, lead, copper, silver, &c.

A short account of the herring fishery—an inexhaustible source of wealth to the islanders—will not prove uninteresting to the reader. The fishing season commences in June, and generally continues until the end of October. Four or five hundred boats, from fifteen to thirty tons burden, are annually employed in this important branch of commerce. The fishermen are scrupulously careful not to leave the harbour on Saturday or Sunday evening. On leaving the shore they use a short prayer. "When the herring-boats proceed to sea, which they do so as to reach the fishing grounds about dusk, they go out in a body, which, from the picturesque appearance of the brown-tanned sails of the boats, is a remarkably pretty spectacle. Arriving at sundown on the spot where the herrings are known to be, the fishermen shoot (the term for lowering) their nets, which is a work of some time. The nets of each boat are about three hundred feet long, and their whereabouts is known to the fishermen by means of long lines of corks, &c., attached to them by ropes, which of course float on the surface of the sea. All the nets hang down curtain-wise in the water, and there is some judgment required in shooting them, as, were they sunk not sufficiently low, the shoal of herrings would often pass beneath them. . . . When it is determined to haul, the first net is examined. If that net contain few or no fish, the whole 'fleet' of nets is allowed to remain longer in the sea; but if, on the contrary, the first net be glittering with its silvery contents, it is reckoned a good omen, and the remainder are hauled in. The sight, if the nets be full of fish, is so extremely beautiful, that, often as we have witnessed it, we are quite powerless to describe it. The whole surface of the sea appears one sheet of molten lead or silver; and if there be a gleam of moonlight the effect is extraordinary. The reader will strive in vain to imagine the appearance of perhaps eighty or one hundred thousand fish in an enormous mass, all held fast by the head, and sparkling like so many lumps of crystal." Great quantities of herring are purchased fresh for transmission to Liverpool; and it is scarcely necessary to remark that vast numbers are consumed in the Isle of Man. As the poet beautifully says—

> "Herring's the food of Mona's greedy sons,
> Who eat them up as fast as butter'd buns!"

The opinion that this fish periodically migrates is rejected by modern authorities. "The herring," says Yarrell, "inhabits the deep waters all around the British coasts, and approaches the shores in the months of August and September for the purpose of depositing its spawn." It can be caught all the year round on the coasts of the three kingdoms. The returns from the produce of the herring fishery of the island average, it is said, about £70,000 per annum. According to *Fun*, fishermen's gains are unquestionably *net* profits!

The circulating medium of the isle consists principally of one-pound notes issued from the insular banks: for the notes put into circulation, the proprietors lodge ample security, in landed property, at the Rolls'-office in Castletown.

The Isle of Man Packet Company possess five splendid and powerful steamers. The *Tynwald*, *Mona's Queen*, *Snaefell*, and *Douglas* ply regularly between Douglas and Liverpool. The *Mona's Isle* plies between Ramsey, Liverpool, and Whitehaven, and during the summer months frequently performs the voyage round the island.

A few remedies for sea-sickness may not be unacceptable to the reader. Some travellers recommend ice as a sure remedy as well as a preventative against this malady, asserting that if the stewards of steamers would keep a supply of lemon-water ices on board, they would profit themselves, and render a great service to their passengers. A recent writer says:—"Camphorated spirit, sal volatile, and Hoffman's ether, a few drops of each, mixed in a small quantity of water, or upon a small lump of sugar, have frequently afforded more relief than all the various remedies extolled for this unpleasant sensation." John Timbs, F.S.A., remarks:—"Anti-putrescent substances have the most powerful influence over this malady, and a little creosote made into a pill is much recommended. In ordinary cases, however, a basin of soup made very hot with cayenne pepper will be found to be effectual." An old traveller observes:—"In all ordinary cases, if in dread of sickness, lie down on the back at least a quarter of an hour before the vessel starts. Let head, body, and back become, as it were, part of the vessel, participating in its motion without muscular effort. Keep yourself warm, as cold induces sickness. For this reason, a little gingerbread is a good thing to eat on board, as it promotes warmth in the stomach. Beware of watching the motion of the vessel, as this has a bad effect on the brain. No position but that of recumbency on the back will do. It will be of little use to assume this position after the sickness has commenced."

The climate of the isle, as already intimated, is remarkable for its exemption of extremes of heat and cold. Provisions are cheap, and house-rent is extremely moderate. We conclude this introductory chapter with the remark that there are now many English residents, who have been attracted by considerations of climate and economy.

CHAPTER II.

CIVIL HISTORY.

"All history, so far as it is not supported by contemporary evidence, is romance."—Dr. JOHNSON.

THE ancient history of the Isle of Man is involved in impenetrable obscurity. Owing to the want of written records, it is very difficult to procure any accurate information concerning the aboriginal inhabitants. Ethnologists and historians have conjectured that the first possessors of the isle were Kelts, of the Gaelic branch.* How it acquired the appellation of Man is uncertain. Antiquaries have amused themselves, with little advantage to others, by suggesting various etymologies of the word, most of them far-fetched and inapplicable. In the time of Cæsar the isle was called Mona :† Ptolemy styled it Μονοειδα, Μόνα Νῆσος, and Μονάρινα; Pliny, Monabia; Orosius, Menavia; Bede, Menavia Secunda; the

---

* "In Ireland, in the Highlands of Scotland, and in the Isle of Man, we have Kelts of the Gaelic, in Wales and Brittany, Kelts of the British branch."—Dr. R. G. LATHAM.— See GIBBON's "Decline and Fall," ch. xxv.

† "In hoc medio cursu est insula quæ appellatur Mona."—De Bello Gallico, lib. v.

Saxons, Mannie; the Welsh, Monaw; the Irish, Manand or Manaind, and Falgach; the Scandinavians, Mön; Nennius, Eubonia; Richard of Cirencester, Moncœda and Manavia: by the natives it is termed Mannin. It is unnecessary in the present day to prove that there is no foundation for the statement that the isle was one of the principal seats of the Druids.

Some writers have supposed that Man was occupied by the Romans. It is asserted that coins of Germanicus and Agrippina have been discovered on the island; and we are gravely assured by Holinshead that in a treaty alleged to have been concluded between Cœsius Nasica and Corbreid, it was stipulated that neither the Scots nor Picts,* from thenceforth should receive or succour, "by anie manner of means, the inhabitants of the Isle of Man, who had done many notable displeasures to the Romans in the last wars!" Nennius affirms that Builc, a Scot, "had the island Eubonia and other adjacent places" in the reigns of Arcadius and Honorius. Little worthy of notice is mentioned of him, except that he murdered and plundered the natives and divided the land between himself and his followers. The next personage alleged by tradition to have reigned in Man was Mannanán mac Lir, a famous necromancer, whose residence was on South Barrull. In the old statute-book of the isle we read:— "Mannanan-Beg-mac-y-Lheirr, the first person who held Man, was the ruler thereof, and after whom the land was named: he reigned many years, and was a paynim. He kept the island under mist by his

---

* "It is certain," says Gibbon, "that in the declining age of the Roman empire, Caledonia, Ireland, and the Isle of Man were inhabited by the Scots; and that the kindred tribes, who were often associated in military enterprise, were deeply affected by the various accidents of their mutual fortunes."—"Decline and Fall," ch. xxv.

necromancy. If he dreaded an enemy, he would cause one man to seem an hundred, and that by art magic." In an ancient Irish glossary—which states that the Isle of Man (Manand) was named after him —he is thus described:—"Manannán mac Lir, *i.e.*, a renowned trader who dwelt in the Isle of Man. He was the best pilot in the west of Europe. Through acquaintance with the sky he knew the quarter in which would be fair weather and foul weather, and when each of these two seasons would change. Hence the Scots and Britons called him a god of the sea, *i.e.*, mac lir, 'son of the sea.'"* An old traditionary ballad, in which his exploits are commemorated, adds this important information:—

> "The rent each landholder paid to him was
> A bundle of coarse meadow grass yearly,
> And that, as their yearly tax,
> They paid to him each midsummer eve!"

There prevails among historians no small discrepancy of opinion as to the precise period at which Manannan lived. According to some authors the celebrated wizard-king flourished three centuries before the birth of Christ! Others affirm that he ascended the throne A.D. 440.

Paulus Orosius (who lived about the middle of the fifth century), after speaking of Ireland, remarks:— "Next to this is the island Menavia, not very little,

---

* "Manannan mac lir. i. cennaige amra bói aninis Manand. isc luam as deach boi aniarthar Eorpa. nofindad tre nemgnacht (i. gnathugud nime) inoiret nobid insoinind & in do[i]nind & intan nosclaechlóbad cechtar don dá résin. inde Scoti et Brittones eum deum vocaverunt maris. et inde filium maris esse dixerunt. i. mac lir mac mara. et de nomine Manandan Inis Manand dictus est."—"Cormac's Glossary." This glossary was written by Cormac Cullionain, King of Munster, and Bishop of Cashel, who was killed at the battle of Bealach Mughna, A.D. 908.

of a good soil, and also inhabited by the Scots."* In
503, according to the "Annals of Ulster," there was
a war in Man. In 520, Maelgwyn, King of North
Wales, and nephew of the illustrious King Arthur,
is said to have made a conquest of the isle from the
Scots. On the demise of Maelgwyn, in 560, the
crown of North Wales and Man devolved upon his
son Rhun. Aydan M'Gabhran, King of Scotland,
invaded the isle in 581, defeated the Welsh, and
established Brendinus, or Brennus, his nephew—a
brave and enterprising prince—in the government.
The latter was soon after slain at Fethanleg, fighting
against the Picts for his uncle. (Abercrombie states
that Brandon, or Brennus, was Lord of Man in 579,
and that he was slain in that year at the battle of
Fethanleg. According to the Anglo-Saxon chronicle,
the battle occurred in 584). In the "Annales
Cambriæ," edited by Rev. J. Williams Ab Ithel,
mention is made, under date 584, of a war against
the Isle of Man, and of the deposition of Daniel of
Bangor. Brennus was succeeded by Eugenius, son
of Aydan. At the death of Aydan, the crown of Scotland devolving upon Eugenius, he, in memory of the
kind reception he had met with in Man, sent his sons,
Ferquard, Fiacre, and Donald, to be educated under
Conanus, bishop of this isle. The Scots appear to
have retained possession of Man until it was subdued
by Edwin, the sovereign of Deira and Bernicia (which
were united under the denomination of Northumbria),
about the year 624. "This Edwin," says the
Venerable Bede, "as a reward of his receiving the
faith . . . received an increase of that which he enjoyed on earth, for he reduced under his dominion all
the borders of Britain that were provinces either of
the aforesaid nation or of the Britons . . . and he in

---

* "Huic etiam Menavia insula proxima est, et ipsa spacio
non parva, solo commodo, æque a Scotorum gentibus habitatur."

like manner subjected to the English the Menavian islands [Anglesey and Man] ... the first whereof, which is to the southward, is the largest in extent, and most fruitful, containing 960 families ... *the other above three hundred.*" In 633 Edwin was slain near Heathfield, in Yorkshire, in battle against the combined kings Cadwalla, of North Wales, and Penda, of Mercia. According to Bede, Edwin's nephew and successor, King Oswald, slew Cadwalla in 635 at Denisbrook (according to Nennius at Catscaul). The former historian asserts that Oswald possessed the sovereignty of the Menavian isles. He was slain, in 642, at Maserfield, by Penda, and the Southumbrians. In the same year Oswy, his brother, succeeded to the kingdom of the Northumbrians, and reigned until 670. He also "held the same dominions for some time, and for the most part made tributary the nations of the Picts and Scots." It is probable that Cadwallader, son of that Cadwalla whom Oswald slew, now obtained possession of the isle. According to the "Annales Cambriæ," a great earthquake occurred in Man in the year 684. Cadwallader was succeeded, in 703, by his son Edwal, who reigned 17 years. In 720, Roderic Maelwynoc succeeded to the throne, and ruled the island until 755. On the demise of Roderic, his eldest son, Cynan Tindaethwy, ascended the throne of Wales. Howel, the brother of the latter king, claimed Anglesey as his portion of his father's inheritance. Cynan disputed this claim, and, in consequence, several battles were fought, and Howel, having been vanquished, was compelled to make his escape to the Isle of Man, which was then under the government of Mervyn Vrych.

About 790, Osred, the son of King Alcred, having unsuccessfully attempted to seize the crown of Northumbria, enrolled himself, to save his life, among the clergy of York, and subsequently, for greater security, fled to the Isle of Man. Some historians assert that Osred was forcibly shaven a monk at York, and not liking a shaven crown, had desired banishment, and was accordingly exiled to the Isle of Man.   Returning from the isle about 793, he braved his rival, Ethelred, to battle, but was deserted by his followers, seized by Ethelred, and cruelly put to death.

Upon the death of Cynan Tindaethwy in 817, Howel, perceiving the Welsh disaffected to him, found it his interest to make up a match between Mervyn Vrych and Essylt—the daughter of Cynan—by which bargain the younger brother of the last-mentioned king obtained the sovereignty of the Isle of Man, the sceptre of North Wales devolving on Mervyn Vrych and Essylt. ·Howel died in 825, and thereupon the isle returned to the possession of Mervyn Vrych.

The annals of Ulster state that in 841 a fleet from the Isle of Man entered the Boyne.   In 843, Bethred, King of Mercia, slew Mervyn Vrych at the battle of Kettle, and, in the same year, Rotri Mawr (Roderic the Great) came to the throne.   About 870 he divided his extensive dominions among his sons Cadel, Aberfyn, and Anaraut, the last of whom obtained the Isle of Man.   Anaraut, the last Welsh king of the isle, was compelled to acknowledge the supremacy of Alfred the Great.   The illustrious monarch of the West Saxons adopted him as his godson, presented him with rich gifts, and caused him to enter into the · same feudal relation with Wessex in which Ethered and Mercia stood.   During the reign of Anaraut, the isle was ravaged by the Norse, who obtained possession of it.   Their first expedition had been directed against Scotland and the Orcades, whence they soon reached the western isles of Scotland, and the Isle of Man.   By degrees these isles became the rendezvous of numerous discontented adventurers

from Norway, who would not submit to the restraints
of Harald Haarfager upon their piratical habits;
and who, from their places of refuge, dared to depre-
date on the coasts of Norway. · This conduct induced
Harald to pursue them to their lurking-places. After
subjugating the Orkneys, the Shetland Isles, and the
Hebrides, the founder of the Norwegian monarchy
proceeded to Man. "When he was come westward
as far as Man," says Harald Haarfager's Saga, "the
report of his exploits on the land had gone before
him; for all the inhabitants had fled over to Scotland,
and the island was left entirely bare both of people
and goods, so that king Harald and his men made no
booty when they landed."* These events probably
occurred about the year 870. A brave Norwegian
baron named Ketil Flatnef (flat-nose), whose daughter
Aude was married to Olave the White, King of
Dublin, is said to have been sent to the isles soon
afterwards by Harald Haarfager to chastise some
vikings who had settled there, although previously
expelled by Harald himself; and Ketil, having
executed his commission, is said to have made himself independent; but Professor Munch is of opinion
that Ketil emigrated from Norway to the isles
because he was obnoxious to King Harald, and that
he was a man of great consequence there long before
the Norwegian monarch proceeded to the isles to
expel the vikings. Harald intrusted the government
of the Sudreys, or Southern Isles, "including no
doubt the Isle of Man," to an earl named Tryggvi,
" and, he having been killed, to another earl named
Asbjörn Skerjablesi. It is, however, obvious that
the position of these earls must have been very pre-

---

* "Ern er hann kom vestr í Mön, tha höfdo their ádr spurt
hvern hernad hann hafdi giört fyrrum thar í landi, thá flýdi
allt folk inn a Scotland, oc var thar aleyda af mönnum: braut
var oc flutt allt fe that er mátti. Enn er their Haralldr
konungr gengu á land, tha fengu their ecki herfang."

carious and dangerous, as they were from Norway, and exposed to incessant attacks from the vikings. Both of them came also to an untimely death; Tryggvi was first killed, as stated above, then Asbjörn was attacked by two relations of Ketil Flatnef, who killed him, captured his wife and daughter, and sold the latter as a slave. There are no traces of King Harald having sent a third earl to the islands" (see Prof. Munch's edition of the "Chronicon Manniæ," pp. 33—35).

Helgi, the son of Ketil, was probably the next king of Man. He was succeeded by Thorstein the Red—Ketil's grandson—who conquered a part of Scotland.

Erik, the son of Harald Haarfager, became chief sovereign of Norway on the death of his father, and ruled that kingdom with so much cruelty that the inhabitants gave him the surname of Blodöxe (Blood-axe). He was expelled from Norway in 934, and proceeded to the Orkneys, where he became a viking, and exercised his depredations on the British coasts. About 948, Northumbria—then peopled with Danes—was conferred upon him by King Athelstane on condition that he and his adherents should abstain from molesting Norway, embrace Christianity, and protect the British shores against the incursions of the Northmen. He was subsequently expelled by the Anglo-Saxons. Soon after, with a band of his former pagan associates, he invaded Northumbria, and was killed in a battle on Stonemoor in the year 950. It is highly probable that this Erik possessed himself of the Isle of Man. He arrived on its shores with a powerful armament, and landed at the Lhane, in the north of Man, where he was met by the islanders. On being asked whence he came, he is said to have replied, pointing to the galaxy, or milky way,—"This is the way to my country:" at the present day that celestial phenomenon is termed by the Manx, *Raad mooar ree Gorree*, or the Great Road of King Orry (see Train's History, vol. i., p. 63). The establishment of the House of Keys is ascribed by tradition to this celebrated pagan king. He is also reported to have divided the island into Sheadings. Erik is the Scandinavian form of the name Enrico, Henricus, and Henry of southern nations. Orry, or Oir-righ,* is merely a Keltic designation, signifying inferior or subordinate king, and is opposed to Ard-righ, or supreme king.

Erik was probably succeeded by his son Gudröd, who, according to tradition, erected Rushen Castle (?). Gudröd's son, Ragnvald, who was reputed a magician, is said to have been the next king. It is said that he attempted to build a bridge from the Point of Ayre, in the Isle of Man, to Burrough Head, in Galloway! In 960 he was succeeded by his son Olaf, after whose death Olain, Allan, Fingall, and Gudröd II., successively ascended the throne. In 973 Hakon (Macon, Maccus, &c.), the son of Harald, became king. He is mentioned among the tributary sovereigns who did homage to King Edgar at Chester, and rowed his barge down the river Dee. Hakon seems to have enjoyed the friendship of King Edgar, who made him admiral of a powerful fleet, with which he sailed round the isles of Britain, in order to clear the seas of the pirates who at that time continually devastated our shores. Sacheverell observes : — "Sir Henry Spelman calls him *totius Angliæ Archipirata*, which in another place he interprets *Prince of Seamen ;* and from him, it is probable, the antient bearing of the island was a ship in her ruff sables, with this inscription, *Rex Manniæ et Insularum ;* which, my author says, was engraved on a seal once in the custody of Mr.

---

* Righ (pronounced rhē) signifies a king or governor.

Camden.   It is certain that coats of arms came to be
used about that time, and this among the critics was
supposed to be the seal of Macon."—(An account of
the Isle of Man, p. 27).   Worsaae, in his Account of
the Danes and Norwegians in England, Scotland,
&c., speaks of "a carved monument erected in the
year 1489 to Lachlan Mackinnon (Mac Fingon), and
on it, underneath the inscription, is a ship, which is
still to be found in the family arms of the Mackinnons,
but which is said to have been originally the heraldic

bearing of the Norwegian kings
in the Isle of Man."   The Rev.
Dr. Wilson, a distinguished
archæologist, remarks :—"The
lymphad, which figures as one of
the heraldic quarterings of the
Mackinnons, is indeed believed
to have been derived from the
Northmen; but in the form it assumes on this and
other Iona sculptures, it bears as little resemblance
to the long-oared war-galley, so frequently engraved
on native Scandinavian ornaments and relics, as the
accompanying ornaments do to any known device of
Northern origin.   The late era to which some of the
most characteristic of those sculptures belong, should
alone suffice to disprove the idea 'that the Scandinavians were the authors of this particular kind of
art exhibited by the stone crosses, as also by the
sepulchral monuments of Argyleshire.'"   Hakon
was killed in 976 by the renowned Brian Boroimhe.
He was succeeded by his brother Gudröd III., who
seems to have been a famous warrior.   In 979 he
supported Constantine the Black against his cousin
Howell, and was twice defeated; but the third time,
on invading Anglesey, he slaughtered 2,000 men,
and obtained possession of that island.   During his
reign the Isle of Man was grievously harassed by
Scandinavian sea-rovers.   Olaf, the piratical son of

Tryggve, King of Norway, proceeded to the Hebrides, where he fought many battles; then southward to Man, where also fought.* Three pirates, named Kara, Grim, and Helga fought with Gudröd, conquered him, and seized much booty.† In 989 they again sailed to Man, fought with and conquered the king, killed Dungal or Donald his son, and obtained an immense booty.‡ In the same year Gudröd III. was slain by the Dalriadic Scots. Ragnvald II. was the next king. Towards the close of the tenth century, the island was a lurking-place of vikings, who year after year made descents on the English coasts. Burning for revenge, King Ethelred the Unready despatched his fleet in 999 to the Isle of Man and depopulated that notorious nursery of pirates. Many of the coins of that celebrated Anglo-Saxon King have been discovered in the Isle.

Ragnvald was succeeded in 1004 by Suibne, who governed Man until 1034, in which year Harald I. ascended the throne. He died in 1040, and Gudröd IV., the son of Sigtrygg, King of Dublin, became king of the isle. After the battle of Stanford-bridge in England, some of the vanquished warriors are said to have fled to the Isle of Man, where they were hospitably received by Gudröd IV. Among these was one Gudröd Crovan or Cronan, according to some the son of Harald the Black of Iceland, or

---

* "Thadan sigldi hann til Sudreya, oc átti thar nockorar orrostor; sidan hellt hann sudr til Manar, oc bardiz thar."— *Olaf Tryggvason's Saga.*

† "Their borduz vid Gudröd konungr or Mon oc sigrudu hann, oc fóru vid that aptr oc höfdu fengit mikit fe," &c.— *Njdlssaga.*

‡ "Tha helldu their til Manar, thar maettu their Gudraudi konungi ur Mani oc borduz their vid hann oc höfdu sigr, oc drapu Dungal son konungs, thar toko their fe mikit," &c.— *Njdlssaga.*

rather Isla, according to others the grandson
of Gudröd III., King of Man. On the death of
Gudröd IV. the sceptre devolved on his son Fingall.
About 1079 Gudröd Crovan conquered Man. (Professor Munch is of opinion that during the interval
between the death of Gudröd III., in 989, and the
accession of Gudröd Crovan about 1079, Man was an
appendage of the Norwegian kingdom of Dublin).
On invading the isle, Gudröd was strenuously opposed
near Scacafell or Skyhill by the forces of the Manx
king Fingall; and in this battle Fingall, and
Sigtrygg, King of Dublin, were slain. It is said
that Gudröd introduced the feudal law into Man.
Professor Munch, however, remarks:—" As the conquest of the Isle of Man by the Norwegians must
have taken place in the 9th century, it is also more
likely that the acquisition of the dominium glebæ by
the conqueror must have taken place then, than afterwards." Gudröd subsequently made himself master
of Dublin and Leinster, and declared himself independent of Norway. In 1093, Magnus Barefoot, *
in order to maintain Norway's right of supremacy
over the isles, undertook his first expedition to the
west. After committing great havoc along the coasts
of Scotland, "he proceeded south towards Cantire,
marauding on both sides in Ireland and Scotland,
and advanced with his foray to Man, and plundered
there as in other places." † According to the sagas,
he expelled Gudröd Crovan, who died in 1095 in
Isla, which island used to be, next to Man, the chief

---

* Magnus is said to have adopted in the mountains of Scotland the national dress of the Highlanders, and hence he
acquired the cognomen of Barfoed, or Barefoot.—*Torfæus,*
tom. iii. lib. vii.

† "Thá fór hann sudr firi Satiri, heriar thar á boedi bord,
á Irland oc Skotland, fór sva allt herskilldi sudr til Manar, oc
heriadi thar sem í ödrom stödom.—*Magnus Barefoot's Saga.*

seat of the kings of Man.* The Jarl Ottar, who was made governor of the isle after Magnus Barefoot's expedition, was deposed by the inhabitants of the southern district, who chose in his place another Jarl named Macmanus or Magnusön (*Worsaae*, p. 288). A civil war ensued. Both parties resolved to terminate the contest by a decisive battle. The people of the south were led by Macmanus, and those of the north by Ottar. An engagement, in which both leaders fell, took place at Sandwath, in Jurby, in the year 1098. The party of Macmanus had nearly gained the victory, when the women of the northern district, rushing to the scene of action, by their opportune assistance, enabled their husbands to defeat the inhabitants of the southern portion of the isle. In the same year Magnus Barefoot reconquered the Scottish isles, where the Norwegian colonists had long been established, but whose jarls had thrown off their dependence on the parent country. Coming to Man, which had been well-nigh depopulated by civil war, he settled colonies on the island, commanded them to build houses, and took care they should be provided with necessaries of every kind.†

Magnus was killed at Moichoaba in 1103, and shortly afterwards Lagman, the eldest son of Gudröd Crovan, ascended the throne of Man. He was succeeded by his brother Olaf III., surnamed Bitlingr (the little bit) or Klining. This monarch married

---

* In an old heraldic MS. in the British Museum, mention is made of " Oland Cronan Roy de Man et . . . qui porte ruby a trois jambes en ung joyntes a genoulles en triangle arme et porte graves et esperons toupase." He is said to have been a son of Gudröd Cronan, or Crovan. It is generally supposed that the three legs were introduced as the arms of Man by Alexander III. of Scotland.

† "Insulam Man quae deserta erat, inhabitavit, populus replevit, domibus et aliis necessariis ad usus hominum gnaviter instruxit."—*Ordericus Vitalis.*

Afreca, daughter of Fergus, Lord of Galloway, and
entered into an amicable alliance with the kings of
England and Ireland. He founded Russin Abbey in
1134. About 1141 Sveinn, the son of Asleif, one of
the most powerful of the Orkney Scandinavian
warriors, assisted his friend Holbud to recover certain
lands in Cornwall. Sveinn joined Holbud at the Isle
of Man; and after a summer spent in piracy on the
coasts of Cornwall, they returned to the Isle of Man,
where Sveinn married Ingerid, the wealthy widow of
a nobleman in Man. After passing the winter in the
island he returned home. In 1154 the three nephews
of Olaf III. (sons of his youngest brother Harald)
demanded half of the isles. Olaf appointed a day
and a place for adjusting the business; and in the
meantime, the three brothers formed a plot to take
away his life. On the day appointed, in the year
1153, the two parties met near Ramsey. Ragnvald,
one of the brothers, taking advantage of Olaf's un-
guarded state, under pretence of saluting him, raised
his battle-axe, and, with one blow, severed the king's
head from his body. The murderers then divided
the island among themselves. Gudröd VI., son of
Olaf, was the next king. The nobility of Leinster
elected him to be their sovereign, rejecting his com-
petitor Ottar, whose son Thorfinn, a man of great
power, persuaded Jarl Somerled, who had some
distant claim to the throne of the isles, to invade
Man. In 1156 a sanguinary engagement took place
in Ramsey Bay between the fleets of Gudröd and
Somerled. Gudröd was compelled to resign to
Somerled all the Sudreyjar from Mull to Man. Two
years afterwards Somerled again invaded the island,
and Gudröd escaped to Norway, where he remained
six years. We learn from the Orkneyinga saga that
in 1159 Sveinn, the son of Asleif, went on a piratical
expedition to the western isles. Thence he proceeded
south to Man; but, not obtaining booty, he then

sailed to Ireland. On the demise of Somerled,
Gudröd VI. returned to Man; but his claim to the
throne was disputed by Ragnvald, (a natural son of
Olaf Klining) whom, however, he defeated. Ragnvald,
son of Ec Margad, subsequently endeavoured to obtain the sovereignty of the isle, and was slain.
Gudröd died in 1187 at Peel Castle, and in the following year his remains were conveyed to Iona, and
deposited in the tomb of the kings of his race.
Gudröd left one legitimate son, Olaf IV., surnamed
the Black, who was thirteen years of age at his
father's death. The Manx, however, constituted
Ragnvald, an illegitimate son, king of the isle. In
1205 he was taken under the protection of John,
king of England, who in 1212 granted him a knight's
fee. Ragnvald III., to liberate himself from doing
homage to the kings of England or Scotland, agreed
to hold his dominions as a fief of the Roman See, on
paying twelve marks sterling annually; and accordingly received investiture of Honorius by a golden
ring in 1219. Olaf the Black, accompanied by Paul
Blakason, came to Man in 1224, and compelled
Ragnvald to cede half the kingdom to him. Shortly
afterwards the latter, under pretence of visiting the
king of England, obtained a large sum of money
from his subjects, in order to defray his expenses, on
receiving which he proceeded to the court of Alan of
Galloway. As Alan was justly regarded by the Manx
as an enemy, this imposition greatly enraged them;
and they forthwith offered the sceptre of the isles to
Olaf. Alan made several descents on Man, and
carried away much booty. Olaf, the swarthy king of
the isle, bravely defended his dominions against the
invader. In 1228, during the absence of Olaf,
Ragnvald, Alan, and Thomas, Earl of Athole,
invaded Man, and after plundering the inhabitants,
returned to Galloway. Ragnvald again invaded the
island in 1229, burnt all the shipping at anchor

under Peel Castle, and in the same year was slain in a battle fought near Tynwald Hill. In 1228 Olaf the Black and Uspak the Norwegian laid siege to Rothesay Castle (in the Isle of Bute), which was taken by storm, after a spirited defence. In 1230 Olaf repaired to Norway, and took the oath of allegiance to King Hacon. Henry III. granted him a knight's fee of corn and wine for defending the sea-coast. He expired at Peel Castle in 1237, leaving three sons (Harald, Ragnvald, and Magnus), and was succeeded by Harald, who, when visiting England in 1246, received a safe conduct from Henry III.* He married Cecilie, daughter of Hakon, king of Norway. On the voyage home in 1248 the royal couple perished in the dangerous Somburg Röst, to the south of Shetland, together with Lawrence, the bishop of the isle, and a numerous retinue of Manx chiefs. Harald's brother, Ragnvald IV., who succeeded to the throne, was shortly afterwards murdered by Harald, son of Gudröd, the knight Ivar, and their accomplices. This unfortunate king left an infant daughter named Mary; but the sceptre of the isles now fell to his youngest brother Magnus, the last of the descendants of Gudröd Crovan, and the last of the Norwegian kings of Man. At the time of Ragnvald's assassination, Magnus being absent from the island, the throne was usurped by Harald, son of Gudröd the Brown, who was summoned to Norway by King Hakon, and, on his arrival, cast into prison (Train, p. 127). In 1250 one John Dulgalson landed at Ronaldsway, proclaiming himself king of the isles; but he and his adherents were defeated and expelled by the Manx. On pro-

---

* "Haraldus, Rex Manniæ habet litteras de conductu in veniendo ad Regem in Angliam, ibidem morando, et redeundo; et durent litterae ad Pentecostem, anno &c. tricesimo. Teste Rege apud Westmonasterium nono die Junii."—*Rymer's Fœdera*, t. i., p. 441.

ceeding to Norway in 1253, Magnus received letters
of safe conduct from the king of England (see
Rymer's Fœdera, t. i., p. 489). In 1263 Hakon, king
of Norway, sailed with a large fleet to avenge the
attack made on the Sudreyjar by the Scots, Magnus
from Man, and Dugald from the Sudreyjar, joining
him at Kerrara. At length Hakon anchored with
his fleet under Cumbrey, opposite the hamlet of
Largs. A fierce battle took place, and the Norwegians were overpowered. Hakon died on the 16th
December, 1263, at Kirkwall. "The kings in Sudreyjar and Man," says Worsaae, "who could no
longer venture to reckon upon adequate protection
from Norway, submitted to the dominion of the
Scotch King. King Magnus Hakonsön, of Norway,
found it most advisible to cede Norway's supremacy
over the Sudreyjar and Man to the Scotch crown for
4,000 marks sterling, and a yearly tribute of 100
marks. But the Scots did not obtain immediate possession of Man. King Magnus died there in 1265,
and was buried in the convent of Russin, near Derby
Haven." "We learn from Fordun," says Professor
Munch, "where the death of Magnus is related,
that he had been married to *filia Eugenii de Ergadia*,
who after his death married Maclise, Earl of Strath-
erne." Ivar, a powerful knight, now assumed the
dominion of the island. "It was not until the year
1270 that the Scots, who had landed at Ragnvalds-
vaag, succeeded, in a hard-fought battle, in killing
Ivar, together with a great number of leading men
of the island, who had fought desperately for their
independence." *

---

* Many names of places in the island which remind us of
the Norwegian dominion, will be specified in subsequent
chapters of this work. The Isle of Man evidently offered
many allurements to the Scandinavians. Magnus Barefoot's
saga states that "Cantire is a great district, better than the
best of the southern isles of the Hebudes, *excepting Man.*—
(Satíri er mikit land, oc er betra enn hin bezta ey í Sudreyom,
nema Mön).

According to tradition, Alexander III., king of
Scotland, erased the ancient armorial bearing of the
Norwegian kings of Man, and substituted the three
legs.   The arms of the island are—*Gules*, three
armed legs, *argent*, conjoined in the fess-point, flexed
in triangle, garnished and spurred, *or*, with the
appropriate motto, *Quocunque jeceris stabit, i.e.,*

Whichever way you throw
it, it will stand.*   This
motto reminds us of a verse
Benvenuto Cellini—a cele-
brated Florentine artist of
the 16th century—carved,
when a youth, round a
mirror.   The mirror was
in the form of a wheel:
round it were seven circles,
in which the seven virtues
were carved in ivory and black bones; and both the
mirror and the figures of the virtues were balanced
in such a manner, that the wheel turning round, all
the virtues moved at the same time, and had a weight
to counterpoise them at their feet, which kept them
in a straight direction.   As he had a smattering of

---

* "The symbol of the three legs conjoined no doubt denotes
the triangular shapes of the Isle of Man and Sicily, or Trinacria.
It is somewhat curious that the earliest coinage of this island,
A.D. 1709 (which by the way is cast, and not struck in the
usual way: obverse, the crest of the Earls of Derby, the eagle
and child, SANS CHANGER; reverse, the three legs), has the
motto QUOCUNQUE GESSERIS STABIT.   The coinage of 1723 is
exactly similar, but struck; whereas that of 1733, and all the
succeeding coinages have QUOCUNQUE JECERIS STABIT, which is
clearly the correct reading."—E. S. TAYLOR, the Numismatist.
"The classical symbol of the island of Sicily (Trinacria) was
formed of three naked legs similarly conjoined, and the triple-
mountained Isle of Man might have awakened in its Norman
sovereigns some recollections of their Mediterranean con-
quests."—PLANCHÉ.

the Latin tongue, he carved a verse round the mirror, the purport of which was "That on which side soever the wheel of fortune turns, virtue stands unshaken upon her feet:" Rota sum semper, quò quò me verto, stat virtus. Mackenzie Walcott, M.A., states that the phrase "right as a trivet" comes probably from the motto of the three-legged stool of Man—Quocunque jeceris stabit" (see *Illustrated London News*, April 5, 1856). A remarkable device of six legs joined at the thighs formed the signature of a clergyman who lived in the fifteenth century—Theodore Brakell, clerk or priest of the diocese of Cologne.

Having conquered the Isle of Man, Alexander III. of Scotland placed successively therein as governors Gudröd Macmanus, Allan, Okerfair, Brennus, and Donald. After his death, various contentions ensued between rival claimants to the throne; and in 1290, when Man was "oppressed with many miseries from lack of protection and defence," Edward I. of England, at the request of the inhabitants, took possession of it (see Rymer's Fœdera, tom. ii., p. 492). In the following year, Mary de Waldebeof, greatgranddaughter of Ragnvald IV., sued for her right before the English king. In 1292 Edward I. commanded John de Huntercombe, to whom the custody of the isle had been committed, to surrender Man to Baliol, king of Scotland. Aufrica — a sister of Magnus, king of Man—thereupon preferred her claim to the sovereignty of the isle, offering to do homage to Baliol; and, not being able to obtain redress from the king of Scotland, she next applied to King Edward, as lord superior. In 1293 Baliol and Aufrica were cited to appear in the King's Bench to have the claim in issue decided there (see Train, p. 144). She was the wife of the English baron, Simon de Montagu, to whom, in 1305, she made over

her right in the island.* It does not appear that
Simon de Montagu, though styled Lord of Man, was
ever seised of the territory.   Sir William Montagu,
son of Aufrica, who married Elizabeth de Montford,
prosecuted the claim of his mother, and wrested the
island from the Scots, whom he drove out of Man.
Having, however, contracted a considerable debt for
this war, and being unable to discharge it, he mort-
gaged the isle to Anthony Beck, bishop of Durham.
Edward II. subsequently bestowed it on Piers
Gaveston—the son of a Gascon knight—whom he
created Earl of Cornwall.   To our Manx readers,
the following extracts from Christopher Marlowe's
tragedy "Edward the Second," will not prove unacceptable :—

"*Edward.* What, Gaveston! Welcome—kiss not my hand—
    Embrace me, Gaveston, as I do thee.
    Why should thou kneel ?
    Know'st not whom I am ?—
    Thy friend, thyself, another Gaveston!

    *   *   *   *   *

    I here create thee lord high-chamberlain,
    Chief secretary to the state and me,
    Earl of Cornwall, king and lord of Man.

Gaveston. My lord, these titles far exceed my worth.

    *   *   *   *   *
    *   *   *   *   *

Lancaster. That villain Gaveston is made an earl.

Old Mortimer. An earl!

---

* To the original deed, by which she gave up her right in
the isle "to her noble and potent husband," her seal is attached.
It contains a full-length portrait of herself, and is very well
executed.   This seal proves her to have been a person of great
consequence, as the *sigillum imaginis* was used by the nobles of
the highest rank only.   Aufrica is styled in several ancient
charters "Heiress of Man" and "Reyne de Man." Her husband is entitled "Roy de Man par sa femme."

Warwick. Ay, and besides lord chamberlain of the realm,
    And secretary too, and lord of Man.

    *   *   *   *   *
    *   *   *   *   *

Edward. My Gaveston! welcome to Tinmouth! welcome to thy
    *   *   *   *   * [friend.
    Will none of you salute my Gaveston ?
Lancaster. Salute him?—yes, welcome, lord chamberlain.
Young Mortimer. Welcome is the good Earl of Cornwall.
Warwick. Welcome, lord governor of the Isle of Man.

In 1308 the isle was given to Henry Beaumont.
Anthony Beck obtained a grant of it for life in 1309,
but in the following year the king resumed possession
of it. Robert Bruce invaded Man in 1313, encountered and routed the governor, stormed Castle
Rushen, and completely subdued the isle, which he
then bestowed on the Earl of Moray. A band of
Irish freebooters, under Richard de Mandeville,
devastated Man in 1316. Martoline—who wrote a
treatise against witchcraft—was sent to the isle in
1329 by the Regent of Scotland, "to take care of
the business of religion, and reformation of manners,
then wholly degenerate" (see Sacheverell, p. 72).
In 1333 William le Taillour, Haver Macoter, and
Gilbert Macstephan, were commanded by King
Edward III. to take possession of Man (see Rymer's
Fœdera, t. iv., p. 558). On the 8th of June in that
year Edward III. committed the custody of the isle to
Sir William Montagu, the grandson of Aufrica,
authorizing him to retain possession until the next feast
of St. Michael, and for one year also from the date of
that feast (see Rymer, t. iv., p. 562). Two months afterwards the king appears to have made over to him all
his rights in the isle (see Rymer, t. iv., p. 574). In
1337 the king created Sir William Montagu—who
was married to Catherine de Grandison—Earl of
Salisbury. Having conquered the island from the

Scots, the earl was crowned king of Man in 1343.*
In the following year he was succeeded by his son,
Sir William Montagu—second Earl of Salisbury of
his family—who married Joan Plantagenet, called the
Fair Maid of Kent, who was divorced on account of
precontract to Sir Thomas Holland. (She was
espoused in 1361 by her cousin, the Black Prince,
by whom she had a son, Richard II., who ascended
the throne of England in 1377). The earl married,
secondly, Elizabeth, daughter of Lord Mohun. In
1393 he sold the isle to Lord Scrope, and died in
1397 without surviving issue, having unfortunately
slain his only son at a tournament at Windsor. In
1397 Beauchamp, Earl of Warwick, was convicted of
high treason; but on account of his submissive
behaviour, his life was spared, and he was banished
to the Isle of Man (Rymer, t. iii., p. 380). The
petition of the Commons, anno 1399, "pur le restitution de Thomas, Counte de Warwic," may be seen in
the Rolls of Parliament, vol. iii., p. 436. Lord
Scrope was decapitated at Bristol in 1399, and the
isle was then granted to the Earl of Northumberland,
to hold by the service of bearing Lancaster's sword

---

* His bravery is commemorated in an old ballad entitled—
"The Winning of the Isle of Man by the noble Earl of Salisbury." We give the first stanza (modernized) :—

> "The noble Earl of Salisbury,
>   With many a hardy knight,
> Most valiantly prepared himself,
>   Against the Scots to fight.
> With his spear and his shield
> Making his proud foes to yield,
> Fiercely on them all he ran,
> To drive them from the Isle of Man,
> Drums striking on a row,
> Trumpets sounding as they go,
> Tan tu ra ra ra tan."

on the left hand of the king at the coronation. On the attainder of the earl, Man was bestowed on Sir John Stanley and his heirs to be held in fee of the king of England, on payment of a cast of falcons at the royal coronation. It does not appear that he ever visited the isle. He greatly distinguished him-self at the battle of Poiçtiers, and married Isabel, heiress of Latham in Lancashire. He was succeeded in 1414 by his son Sir John Stanley, who, finding that the laws of the island were unwritten, caused them to be committed to writing, and to be promulgated from Tynwald Hill. He introduced into Manx legislation all the reforms which the necessities of the age seemed to require—reforms which produced important and highly beneficial consequences (see the " Stanley Legislation of Man," by the Rev. W. Mackenzie). Stanley died in 1432. His son and successor, Thomas (whom Henry VI. created Baron Stanley), ruled the isle until 1459. He was succeeded by Thomas, his son, who crowned the Earl of Richmond immediately after the battle of Bosworth Field, proclaiming him king by the name of Henry VII. That monarch raised Lord Stanley to the dignity of Earl of Derby. Dying in 1504, his grandson, Thomas, succeeded to the title of Earl of Derby and King of Man. He governed the island until 1522. His son, Edward, was placed in positions of highest trust and influence in the reigns of Henry VIII., Edward VI., Mary, and Elizabeth. " With Edward, Earl of Derby's death," says Camden, " the glory of hospitality seemed to fall asleep." Henry, the fourth earl, who succeeded his father in 1572, was one of the commissioners who sat on the trial of the unfortunate Mary, Queen of Scots. He died in 1594.

The Fortune Theatre—the oldest in London—was partly rebuilt about 1599 by Alleyn the famous actor

and founder of Dulwich College, on land belonging
to several Manxmen.*

On the death of the fourth earl, his son Ferdinand
succeeded to the titles and estates. He was married
to Alice, daughter of Sir John Spencer, of Althorp in
Northamptonshire. When that lady became countess
dowager of Derby, she resided in the neighbourhood
of Horton in Buckinghamshire. Milton lived for
some time at Horton, and the "Arcades" was performed by the grand-children of the countess at
Harefield-place. "It seems to me," says Todd,
"that Milton intended a compliment to his fair
neighbour,—for fair she was,—in his 'L'Allegro' :—

> 'Towers and battlements it sees,
> Bosomed high in tufted trees,
> Where, perhaps, some beauty lies,
> The cynosure of neighbouring eyes.'

The woody scenery of Harefield, and the personal
accomplishments of the countess, are not unfavour-
able to this supposition." Ferdinand died in 1594 in
the flower of his youth, "and some suspected," says
Kennet, "he was poisoned. . .His brother William

---

* "It cost £520 for its erection, as appears from the following memorandum in his handwriting in one of his pocket-
books :—

'What the Fortune cost me, Nov. 1599 :

First, for the leas to Brew	£240
Then for building the playhouse . . .	520
For other private buildings of myn owne . .	120

So it hath cost me in all for the leasse . . £880

Bought the inheritance of the land of the Gills of the Isle of
Man within the Fortune, and all the howses in Whight Cross
Street and Goulding Lane, in June 1610, for the some of £340.

Bought in John Garret's lease in reversion from the Gills,
for 21 years, for £100. So in all it cost me £1320.

Blessed be the Lord God everlasting.' "—(See "An Account of
Theatres in Shakespeare's Time," p. 45).

enjoyed after him the honour and title of Earl of
Derby, who had afterwards a trial with the three
daughters of the Lord Ferdinand, for the dominion
of the Isle of Man. The Queen, being sensible that
the English fugitives and the Spaniards had an eye
upon that isle, committed the government of it to Sir
Thomas Gerard, knight, for his approved loyalty, and
by reason of his near neighbourhood thereto, till the
claim should be determined (Hist. of Eng., vol. i.,
p. 580). Before the controversy had been determined by law, King James bestowed the isle on the
Earl of Northampton and the Earl of Salisbury (see
Dr. Oliver's Monumenta, vol. iii., p. 88). The controversy was at length decided in favour of the
daughters of the late earl (see Monumenta, vol. iii.,
p. 91). William was thereupon compelled to come
to an agreement with the successful litigants for the
purchase of their claims and interest in the Isle of
Man (see Seacombe, p. 177). In 1609 the isle was
granted to him by James I., and in the following year
that grant was confirmed by an Act of Parliament.
In 1637, after bestowing Man on his son James, he
retired to a small seat near Chester, where he died in
1642. James, the seventh earl, zealously interested
himself in the royal cause during the civil wars.
His intrepid countess—a daughter of the illustrious
house of Tremouille in France—defended Latham
House for two years against the parliamentary forces.
In 1645 Lord Digby, after his defeat at Sherborne,
fled to the Isle of Man, and thence to Dublin. Four
years afterwards Cromwell's son-in-law, Ireton, endeavoured to induce the earl to deliver up the isle,
but the stern and gallant royalist indignantly rejected
the proposals of the commissary-general, remarking
in his letter—"If you trouble me with any more
messages, I will burn the paper and hang the
bearer!" In 1651 a small ship having been driven
into Ayr harbour and searched by Cromwell's garri-

son, "discloses a matter highly interesting to the Commonwealth. A plot on the part of the English Presbyterian-royalists, English royalists proper, &c. . to unite with the Scots and their king. .The little ship was bound for the Isle of Man, with tidings to the Earl of Derby concerning the affair" (see Carlyle's Letters, &c., of Cromwell, vol. ii., p. 125). In the same year Charles II. sent an express to the earl "that he should meet his majesty in Lancashire." He accordingly met the king, who in his first year had sent him the garter; "which,. in many respects, he had expected from the last. And the sense of that honour made him so readily comply with the king's command in attending him, when he had no confidence in the undertaking, nor any inclination to the Scots. . . .He was a man of great honour. and clear courage; and all his defects and misfortunes proceeded from his having lived so little time among his equals, that he knew not how to treat his inferiors" (see Clarendon's Hist. of Rebellion, b. xiii). Massey, a Presbyterian officer in Lancashire, was joined by the earl with 60 horse and 260 foot from the Isle of Man. In the meantime Cromwell had despatched Colonel Lilburne, with his regiment of horse, into that county. The royalist and parliamentary forces met near Wigan. An engagement took place, and the king's troops were defeated. The earl was subsequently taken prisoner. "He offered to surrender his Isle of Man in exchange for his life, and petitioned for 'his grace the lord general's and the parliament's mercy.' But his petition was not delivered by Lenthal before it was too late. It was read in the house on the eve of his execution, which took place at Bolton, in Lancashire, Oct. 15, 1651" (see Lingard's Hist. of Eng.) "The same night," says Clarendon, "one of those who was amongst his judges sent a trumpet to the Isle of Man, with a letter directed to the Countess of Derby, by by which he required her "to deliver up the castle and island to the parliament." Soon after the execution of this unfortunate nobleman, an effort was made by many of the islanders to induce the Countess of Derby to modify certain arrangements—relating chiefly to tenures—which had been introduced by her husband. (With a view to benefit himself pecuniarily, James, the seventh earl, seems to have compelled the landholders to surrender their estates and to accept leases of 21 years' duration). William Christian, the receiver-general, who headed this insular movement—afterwards absurdly termed an insurrection—strongly urged the countess to consent to the proposition of the islanders. Man was surrendered to the parliamentary forces in the same year (1651) and granted to Lord Fairfax, who generously paid all the rents of the isle into the hands of the Countess Dowager of Derby.* After the Restoration,† the son of the late earl ordered William Christian to be proceeded against "for all his illegal actions at, before, and after the year 1651," charging him with being the head of an insurrection against the Countess of Derby in 1651, "assuming

---

* "The Duke [of Buckingham] heard how kind and generous my Lord Fairfax was to the Countess of Derby, in paying all the rents of the Isle of Man, which the parliament had also assigned to him, for his arrears, into her own hands, and she confessed it was more than all her servants before had done."— *Annual Register*, vol. ii., p. 300.

† The following is taken from a parish register in the Isle of Man:—"Charles the Second, by the grace of God, King of England, &c. . . .was proclaimed in the Isle of Man, in Peeltown, at the Cross, May 20th; at Castletown Cross, May 29th; At Douglas Cross, May 30th; and at Ramsey Cross, May 31st, 1660, with shouting, shooting of musketry and ordnance, drinking of beer, with great rejoicing, the Governor, James Chaloner, being at the said places attended with the officers, civil and spiritual, 24 Keyes, the captains of the parishes, and above 60 horse, besides the officers" (see *Manx Sun*, Mar. 11, 1865).

the power unto himself, and depriving her ladyship,
his lordship, and heirs thereof." Christian's defence
seems to have been comprised in a written declaration which he presented to his judges—a document
that was never permitted to be published, and
which was probably destroyed. Seeing that he was
a marked victim of his persecutors, who were determined to shed his blood, he pleaded the virtue of
Charles the Second's general pardon as a bar against
all the charges which were preferred against him.
This plea the Manx court presumptuously and
illegally held to be " of no efficiency in the case of
treason against a member of the reigning family,"
and accordingly William Christian, the patriotic
Manxman, was judicially murdered on the 2nd of
January, 1663, meeting death with distinguished
fortitude.   It has been asserted that on the appearance of the parliamentary forces in 1651, " Christian
treacherously seized Lady Derby and her family at
midnight, and next morning conveyed them prisoners
to Duckenfield."   Suffice it to say that had this tale
" rested on the slightest semblance of truth, we
should inevitably have found an attempt to prove it
in the proceedings of this mock trial " (see Historical
Notices of Two Characters in Pev. of Peak, by
Colonel Wilks, p. 28).   Several equivocal authorities
have endeavoured to blacken Christian's reputation ;
but no credible evidence has ever been adduced in
support of their allegations.   " Edward Christian,
the nephew, and George, the son of the deceased,"
says Colonel Wilks, " lost no time in appealing to
his majesty in council against this judicial murder. . .
the governor, deemster, &c., were brought up to
London by a serjeant-at-arms, and. . .together with
the Earl of Derby, being compelled to appear, a full
hearing took place before the king in person, the
chancellor, &c. . .judgment was extended on the 5th
August, and that judgment was on the 14th of the

same month ordered "to be printed in folio. . .and his Majesty's Arms prefixed." "This authentic document," continues Colonel Wilks, "designates the persons brought up as 'Members of the pretended court of justice;' declares 'that the general Act of Pardon and Amnesty did extend to the Isle of Man, and ought to have been taken notice of by the judges in that island, *although it had not been pleaded;* that the court refused to admit the deceased William Christian's plea of the Act of Indemnity, &c. Full restitution is ordered to be made to his heirs of all his estate, &c. . .And to the end that the blood that has been unjustly spilt may in some sort be expiated, &c. . .the deemsters are ordered to be committed to the King's Bench to be proceeded against, &c. . .and receive condign punishment" (see Col. Wilks's Hist. Notices, pp. 36—38).

In Head and Kirkman's rare work (published in 1668) entitled "The English Rogue Described," the "rogue" is shipwrecked on the Isle of Man. The following is an extract:—"We stay'd about a week in this Isle of Man without one farthing expense. For the inhabitants are very civil and courteous, and especially to strangers." Charles, the eighth Earl of Derby, died in 1672, and was succeeded by his son William, who appointed Dr. Wilson to the Bishopric. In an account of the services done at the coronation of James II., and his Queen, in 1684, it is stated that— "The Earl of Derby, as seised in fee of the Isle and Castle of Pelham, and dominion of Man, claimed to present the king with two faulcons on this day: which was allowed, and the faulcons presented accordingly" (see Annual Reg., vol. iv., p. 204). The famous siege of Londonderry occurred in 1689. General Kirke was despatched from Liverpool with reinforcements for the relief of the besieged inhabitants. "On the sixteenth of May," says Lord Macaulay, "Kirke's troops embarked: on the

twenty-second they sailed : but contrary winds made
the passage slow, and forced the armament to stop
long at the Isle of Man" (see The Hist. of Eng., vol.
iii., p. 225).   James, the tenth Earl of Derby,
assumed the reins of government in 1702.   In the
following year, chiefly through the influence of
Bishop Wilson, the Act of Settlement, which has
been appropriately styled the Manx *Magna Charta*,
was obtained.   It terminated all disputes concerning
tenures.   "The people obtained a full recognition of
their ancient rights, on condition of doubling the
actual quit rents, and consenting to alienation fines,
first exacted by the Earl James in 1643."   On the
demise of the tenth earl, in 1735, the male line of
Earl William failing, James, Duke of Athole, succeeded to the isle as heir-general by a female branch.
He was married to Lady Amelia Sophia Stanley, the
third daughter of the seventh Earl of Derby. Though
the title of king of Man had long been disused,
the earls of Derby, as lords of the isle, had maintained a sort of royal authority therein by assenting
or dissenting to laws, and exercising an appellate
jurisdiction.   But the distinct jurisdiction of this little
royalty having been found inconvenient for the purposes
of public justice, and for the revenue, it affording a
commodious asylum for debtors, outlaws and smugglers
authority was given to the Treasury, by statute, 12
Geo. I., c. 28, to purchase the interest of the then
proprietor, the Earl of Derby, for the use of the
Crown. Proposals were accordingly made to Lord
Derby, and afterwards to the Duke of Athole; but
the object of government was not attained for many
years.   On the decease of the latter nobleman in
1764, John, the male heir of the dukedom, who was
married to his cousin Charlotte, only child of the late
duke, became possessed of the Isle of Man in
right of his wife; and proposals for the purchase
were immediately made to them by the Treasury.

The purchase was at length effected in 1765 (the duke and duchess reluctantly accepting £70,000, and an annuity of £2,000 for their rights in the isle), and confirmed by statutes 5 Geo. III., c. 26 and 39, whereby the whole island and its dependencies, except the landed property of the Athole family, their manorial rights and emoluments, and the the patronage of the bishopric and other ecclesiastical benefices, were unalienably vested in the Crown, and subjected to the regulations of the British excise and customs. Further sums were subsequently paid to the dukes of Athole * (see Chapter I). John Wood, Esq., the first regal Governor, took possession of the regalities of Man for his Majesty George III. on the 11th of July, 1765. "At a general convention of the estates and legislature of the Isle of Man [July, 1770], being the first high court of Tynwald that has been holden there under the auspices of his present majesty, since the regalities of Man and the isles have been annexed to the Crown of Great Britain, the bishop and clergy of the diocese presented an address to his excellency, John Wood, Esq., the Governor, in which they congratulated his excellency on the royal favour of being commissioned by his majesty to the vicegerency of that island, and express their joy at seeing their ancient, supreme, constitutional, and so much wished-for court of Tynwald, restored to its former or rather superior lustre and importance; and conclude with earnest supplications that his majesty may never want so faithful a representative, the church so sincere a friend, or that island so acceptable a Governor."

The Governor concludes his answer in a happy imitation of Shakespeare :—

"Your applause, my lord, reflects a virtue on myself, and makes me proud indeed!"

---

* "The island was held *in petty serjeanty* by the Athole family, and no definition of *sovereignty* will reach the Lords of Man" (see Lord Ellenborough's speech, July, 1805).

To the archdeacon and clergy he said : — "To
deserve your esteem has ever been my peculiar study ;
to preserve it shall be my constant care. The same
wise Providence which has inspired your goodness,
will, I doubt not, teach me, as far as I am able, to
encourage and reward its labours" (see Annual Reg.,
vol. xiii., p. 126). All that the Revesting Act did
was to transfer the sovereignty from the Lord Proprietor to the King. It made no other change in the
Constitution than what that transfer necessarily occasioned. His Majesty became invested with all the
authority, both legislative and executive, that the
lord had formerly enjoyed, and as the functions of
the other branches of the legislature remained un-
altered, laws continued to be made and promulgated
almost entirely in the same manner that they had
been before. John, the third Duke of Athole, died
in 1774, and was succeeded by his son, of the same
name. At the coronation of George IV. in 1821, the
last honorary service of presenting two falcons was
rendered by the duke in person, and, four years
afterwards, all his manorial rights in the isle were
purchased by the lords of the Treasury for the use of
the Crown. In 1805 Colonel Smelt was appointed
Lieutenant-Governor. He was succeeded in 1832 by
Colonel Ready, who died in 1845. His successor
was the Hon. Charles Hope—uncle to the Earl of
Hopetoun—on whose resignation, in 1860, Francis
Pigott, Esq., Member of Parliament for Reading, was
constituted Lieutenant-Governor. Dying in 1863, he
was succeeded by Henry Brougham Loch, Esq., C.B.
In noticing the appointment of this gentleman to the
governorship of the isle, the *Times* congratulated the
inhabitants upon obtaining " a man of energy who
has seen military and diplomatic services in all parts
of the world." In 1857 he accompanied the Earl of
Elgin on his mission to China as first attaché, and
was selected by that distinguished nobleman to convey to England the treaty with Japan, signed in

1858. On his return to China he acted as private secretary to Lord Elgin. It will be remembered that Sir Hope Grant exacted from the Emperor of China the sum of £100,000 for the murders and other atrocities perpetrated upon the English at Pekin. For the cruelties and confinement to which Mr. Loch was subjected in China, compensation was awarded him to the amount of £8,000. Of his administrative capacity Manxmen have had abundant proof. The worthy Lieutenant-Governor, who was married in 1862 to a niece of the Earl of Clarendon, is indefatigable in his efforts to promote the prosperity of the Isle of Man.

CHAPTER III.

ECCLESIASTICAL HISTORY.

" During all ages, no philosophy, or sect, or religion, or law, or discipline, has been found which so highly exalted the public good. . .as the holy Christian faith."—LORD BACON.

HISTORY does not supply us with any minute or satisfactory information respecting the religion of the aboriginal inhabitants of Man.* According to tra-

---

* " Very little information is to be procured on the mode of worship practised by the pagan Irish. The Danaans reverenced Mananan Lir, Chief of the Isle of Man, and the beneficent patron of sea-faring people. The early missionaries had some trouble to suppress the devotions offered to him. . .As our knowledge of the peculiar mythology of the ancient Celts is far from extensive or satisfactory, it is not out of place here to quote the opinion of a section of our living archæologists, viz., that beast worship prevailed to some extent. . .The number of places in the country named from animals is very great."—*Dub. Univ. Mag.*, Nov., 1863.——In the Isle of Man we have Slieau Whuaillan (Mountain of the Whelp), Cronk-y-Voddey (Hill of the Dog), &c.

dition, the Druids possessed great authority in the isle. Many well-known writers have asserted that it was one of their principal seats; but, that this statement is very apocryphal, few in the present day will venture to deny. Evidence supplied by the researches of archæologists abundantly proves that the stone circles which are scattered over the island, and which have been generally supposed to be Druidical temples, belong to low graves, whose date is of the latest period of heathenism, or what is called the Iron Age (see Worsaae's "Danes and Northmen," p. 233).

Most authors have ascribed the first knowledge of the true faith in the Isle of Man, to the preaching of St. Patrick, who, it is affirmed, was cast ashore on the Manx islet which bears his name. The history of the tutelary saint of Ireland is mixed up with so much romance as to render it extremely difficult to separate truth from fable. It appears that by "his unceasing labours, his powerful eloquence, and the astonishing miracles which he wrought," Saint Patrick—if ever there was such a man*—converted some of the inhabitants to Christianity. At this time, it seems, Manannan mac Lir—the celebrated necromancer—ruled in Man: "the which Manannan was after conquerid by St. Patryke of Irelande who slew all of that ysle which forsooke not their sorcery, and christenid the rest" (see Dr. Oliver's Monumenta, vol. i., p. 84). He is also reported to have founded a church on the islet to which allusion has been made, and after a sojourn of three years to have departed in 447, constituting St. Germanus bishop of the isle. This prelate, to whom the Cathedral in Peel Castle is dedicated, is said to have firmly established the Christian religion in the island. A

---

* "Suppose that St. Patrick, for example, *if ever there was such a man*, had not the true apostolical orders," &c.—*Macaulay's Essays*, p. 74.

ballad, which was composed in the sixteenth century,
says :—

> "For each four quarterlands he made a chapel
> For people of them to meet to prayer;
> He also built German Church, in Peel Castle,
> Which remaineth there until this day."

After the decease of St. Germanus, St. Patrick successively sent Conindrius and Romulus to fill the
episcopal office (see Sacheverell, p. 109). The next
bishop was Maccaille, or Maughold, who, it is
affirmed, divided the island into parishes, and caused.
a church to be erected in each. St. Bridget is stated
to have visited Man to receive the veil from the hands,
of its distinguished bishop. Chambers says :—" She
was renowned for her beauty. To escape the temp-
tations to which this dangerous gift exposed her, as
well as the offers of marriage with which she was
annoyed, she prayed God to make her ugly. Her
prayer was granted ; and she retired from the world
. . .and devoted herself to the education of young
girls."* Maccaille was succeeded in 518 by Lomanus.
Conchan was constituted bishop in 540. His successor was St. Rooney. Conanus, under whose care
the princes of Scotland were placed, was the next
bishop. In 648 he was succeeded by Contentus, after
whose decease Baldus and Malchus were successively
raised to the episcopal dignity. Extreme obscurity
overhangs the ecclesiastical history of the isle from
about the year 700 to the year 1025. No authentic
records of the Manx Church during that period are
extant. From the close of the ninth to about the
end of the tenth century, during which time the

---

* "There was a monastery in the Ile of Mona, where S.
Bridget. . .with three other virgins at one time became nunnes,
being professed by Machillas, then bishop. . .She was first
buried in Mona, and her body translated to Dune in Ireland in
the year 518."—*Broughton's Eccl. Hist.*, p. 605.

island was possessed by pagan Northmen, probably
there was no succession of bishops. The lawless
habits of the Scandinavians, and their invincible
attachment to the ancient idolatry of the North,
would ·present formidable obstacles to their conver-
sion. An old tradition asserts that a temple, dedicated
to Thor, stood on the site of the church of St. John the
Baptist, near Tynwald Hill. It appears, however,
that Christianity must have been disseminated among
the Scandinavian inhabitants of Man at the commencement of the eleventh century.* Brandinus, or
Brandon, occupied the bishopric in 1025. The church
of Braddan, near Douglas, is dedicated to this prelate. He was succeeded in 1050 by Roolwer (Rolf?)
after whose demise William filled the see. His successor was Aumund M'Olaf. In the year 1100
Vermundus was elected bishop. He was the first
who held the combined sees of Sodor and Man.†
This prelate was succeeded by John, a monk of Sais,
who was interred in St. German's Cathedral. Gamaliel
was made bishop in 1154. In 1177 Cardinal Vivian
was sent to Man to see the king married in proper

---

* "The Northmen on the Isle of Man were. . .at a very
·early period Christians. Almost all the Manx Runic stones are
·ornamented with the Christian cross ; and on a defaced piece
·of such a monumental stone we even find the words Jesus
Christ (Jsu Krist). From the language of the inscriptions there
is reason to suppose that they were for the most part engraved
in the eleventh century. We cannot therefore doubt that
Christianity must at that time have been already disseminated
among the Scandinavian population in the Isle of Man."—
Worsaae's "Danes and Northmen," p. 286.

† "The previously distinct bishoprics of the Sudreyjar
(founded in 838) and of Man were united after Magnus Barfod's
expedition, and connected more closely than ever with Norway,
by being subjected to the archbishopric of Trondhjem. From
1181 until 1334 the bishops of the Sudreyjar ('Episcopi
Sodorenses') were consecrated by the archbishop of Trondhjem.
In the year 1380 the bishopric of Man was again separated

form—Gudröd's marriage with Phingola not having
taken place according to the rights of the Catholic
Church. The king, on this occasion, presented to the
Church a portion of the land of Mireskog—near
Ramsey—where he built a monastery. Subsequently
this donation was transferred to the Abbey of Rushen
(see Train, vol. i., p. 107). Ragnvald, a Norwegian,
occupied the see in 1181. It is stated that the
insular clergy granted to him a third of the tithes
"that in after times they might be free from all
demands of the bishops." He was succeeded in
1190 by Christian of Argyle. In 1195, Michael, a
native of Man, "was for his mildness, gravity, and
eminent qualities, raised to the episcopal dignity."
His successsr was Nicholas de Meux, after whom
came Ragnvald, nephew to Olaf the Black. He was
succeeded in 1226 by John Haarfarson, who, by an
accident arising from the negligence of his servants,
was burnt to death. Simon, "a man well read in
the holy scriptures," was consecrated bishop in 1230.
He was buried in Peel Cathedral, which he had
begun to erect. In 1246, Harald, King of Man,

---

from that of the other Sudreyjar; but the subsequent bishops
of Man have retained to the present day the old title of bishop
of Sodor (and Man), taken originally from Sudreyjar.

"About the time that the proper Sudreyjar were, with regard
to ecclesiastical matters, united with Man, many of them were, as
to secular government, separated from that island, although,
since the time of Harald Haarfager, all had been governed by
the same kings."—*Worsaae.*

The same authority remarks:—"All the islands along the
west coast, from Lewis to Man, were called under one name
'Sudreyjar,' or the *southern* islands, from their situation with
regard to the Orkney and Shetland Isles. Sometimes, however, they did not reckon Man among them, and then divided
the rest of the islands into two groups, in such a manner that
only the islands to the south of Mull were called 'Sudreyjar,'
whilst Mull itself, and the islands to the north, obtained the
name of 'Nordreyjar.'"

granted to the monks of Furness "in free alms" the use of all mines which might be found in the isle (see Monumenta, vol. ii., p. 79). Lawrence was the next bishop. He was drowned in 1248. Richard, an Englishman, succeeded him, and ruled the see excellently for twenty-three years. He consecrated the Abbey Church of St. Mary of Rushen. In 1275 Marcus, a Scotchman, was constituted bishop. When the Regent of Scotland surrendered that kingdom into the hands of the King of England, Marcus, says Mackintosh, "had the infamy to bring the first fruits of servility to the feet of Edward, and was the only prelate who swore the oath of fealty on the first day." In 1291 he held a synod at Kirk Braddan, where thirty-five canons were enacted (see Sacheverell, p. 114). In 1292 three justices were sent to Man to hear and determine the complaints of the inhabitants (see Monumenta, vol. ii., p. 121). Marcus was succeeded by Onanus, after whom came Mauritius. Allan, Vicar of Arbory, next filled the see, "with great approbation." He was followed by Gilbert of Galloway, Bernard, and Thomas. Thomas died in 1348. William Russell, Abbot of Rushen, was the next bishop. He was elected by the whole clergy of Man, in St. German's Cathedral. "He was consecrated by Pope Clement the VI. at Avignon; and was the first that shook off the yoke of the Archbishop of Drontheim, by whom his predecessors had for many ages been consecrated" (see Sacheverell, p. 115). This prelate founded a house of minor friars at Beemacken near the Abbey of Rushen. His successor was John Duncan, a Manxman, who was elected in 1374. He was subsequently confirmed by Gregory XI. Robert Waldby was constituted bishop in 1380, in which year the see of Man was again separated from that of the other Sudreyjar. In 1402 John Sprotton was raised to the episcopal dignity. The patronage of the see was granted in 1407 to Sir

John Stanley; and from that period the bishops were nominated by the Lords of Man. In 1429 Richard Pulley was promoted to the see. He was succeeded in 1448 by John Green. In 1452 Thomas Burton was consecrated bishop. Richard Oldham was appointed to the see in 1481. His successor was John Hesketh. In 1505 the lands and privileges which anciently belonged to the bishops of the isle were confirmed to this prelate and his successors, by Thomas, Earl of Derby. Thomas Stanley was appointed to the see in 1542, when the Act 33 Henry VIII., cap. 31 (by which the bishopric was separated from the province of Canterbury and declared to be within the province of York) came into operation. For opposing this measure he was deposed. His successor was Robert Ferrar, who was subsequently translated to the see of St. David's. In the reign of Queen Mary he was burnt at the stake for his Lutheran opinions. Henry Mann was appointed to the bishopric in 1546. In 1556 Thomas Stanley re-obtained his bishopric, and was constituted Governor of Man. His successor was John Salisbury, who died in 1573. John Merrick, who drew up the account of the island published in Camden's "Britannia," was the next bishop. In a letter to the celebrated antiquary, this prelate asserts that the Manx "abhor the civil and ecclesiastical dissensions of the neighbouring countries. There never were any religious feuds in the island, but there never were any penal or incapacitating laws to create them, or impede the inhabitants from worshipping their Maker in the form which their consciences dictate." George Lloyd succeeded to the see in 1600. He was followed in 1605 by John Phillips. In 1633 William Foster was raised to the episcopal dignity. Two years afterwards he was succeeded by Dr. Richard Parr, who is said to have been a notorious gamester. This prelate died in 1643, and the see remained

vacant until 1661. In 1652 Parliament granted the
lordship of the island to Lord Fairfax. Episcopacy
having been abolished, that nobleman generously
applied the revenues of the bishopric to the support
of the clergy, and the maintenance of free schools at
Douglas, Ramsey, Peel, and Castletown. "Considering the ministers here are generally natives,"
says Chaloner, "and have had their whole education
in this isle, it is marvailous to hear what good
preachers there be" (see Chaloner, p. 8). The
Manx of the seventeenth century delighted in music.
"For recreation they are so addicted to the violin
that there is scarce any family but is provided there-
with" (see Blome's "Britannia"). Several writers
have asserted that Lord Fairfax was a persecutor of
the Quakers who settled in Man. It is highly probable that these "persecuted" followers of Penn
introduced the indecorous "manners and customs"
of their English brethren. Speaking of the English
Quakers of that period, Hume says:—"A female
Quaker came naked into the church where the Protector sat; being moved by the Spirit, as she said, to
appear before the people; a number of them fancied
that the renovation of all things had commenced,
and that clothes were to be rejected, together with
other superfluities. The sufferings which followed
the practice of this doctrine, were a species of persecution not well calculated for promoting it." In
1660, Edward Hyde, Earl of Clarendon, wrote from
Brussels to Dr. John Barwick, urging him to accept
the bishopric of Man. The following is an extract
from his letter:—"I cannot blame you for not being
desirous of accepting the bishoprick of Man; which
if you should do, nobody will accuse you of ambition.
. . .The King bids me tell you, that as he doth intend
you a much better preferment, so if it be found
necessary that you submit to this for the present
service, you shall not continue in it after his Majesty

shall be able to remove you from it. . .and since the
election for Man is in my Lord of Derby, and he hath
confer'd it upon you, and much time may be spent in
the alteration, I hope your friends will persuade you
to accept of it for the facilitating the rest " (Kennet's
Register, &c., p. 54). "When the Right Hon. the
Countess Dowager of Derby desired Dr. Barwick to
give up the right he had to the bishoprick of the
Isle of Man; since, as she said, he might hope for
better preferment from his Majesty, and her ladyship
was very desirous, if he would give way, to prefer
her chaplain, Mr. Samuel Rutter, to that diocese,
Dr. Barwick readily comply'd with her request, much
rejoiced that it was in his power to oblige so great a
person " (Kennet, p. 302). Samuel Rutter was
accordingly consecrated bishop in 1661. He was
interred in Peel Cathedral, and succeeded by Dr.
Barrow, who was also made Governor of Man. His
successor was Dr. Bridgeman. Dr. Lake was made
bishop in 1682. He was one of the six prelates who
were committed to the Tower of London by James II.
Dr. Levinz succeeded to the see in 1684. The celebrated Dr. Thomas Wilson was constituted bishop in
1697. This excellent prelate induced the Earl of
Derby to grant the Act of Settlement. The good
bishop's zeal occasionally involved him in difficulties.
He ordered a copy of the "Independent Whig" to
be carried off from a public library because he supposed it to be inimical to "the true government of
the Church;" but the Governor compelled him to
restore it. In 1729 he was involved in a more serious
dispute. Mrs. Horne, the Governor's wife, having
cast aspersions on the character of Sir J. Pool and
on that of a Mrs. Puller, the Governor's chaplain
debarred her from the sacrament. That lady and
Sir J. Pool were cleared of the charges by the bishop,
who thereupon sentenced Mrs. Horne to ask pardon
of them; and she declining to do so, the bishop

debarred Mrs. Puller from the sacrament. The chaplain, however, received her at the communion, and, in consequence, was suspended by his diocesan. He appealed to the civil power, and the Governor fined the bishop £50, and his vicars-general £20 each. As they refused to pay these fines, they were committed to the prison of Castle Rushen, where they were confined two months. The King reversed all the Governor's proceedings, and, to reimburse the bishop, offered him the see of Exeter, which, however, he declined to accept. Bishop Wilson was a rigid disciplinarian. Many curious details of the early form of church discipline, including recitals of the forms of penance enjoined in each case, may be found in the Rev. Dr. Keble's life of that apostolic prelate. "We have instances of men," says Mr. Keble, "censured for 'fiddling' on Sunday, which is called 'a crime,' or even on Saturday night. A churchwarden of Ballaugh presents himself for sending a messenger to Castletown on Whit-Sunday. At Douglas, 1724, a man was censured for shaving in church-time on a Sunday; and another for swimming a duck with a spaniel as he came from the parish church on Sunday evening. In more than one instance persons are presented for sleeping in church, and promise repentance" (see Keble, vol. i., p. 352). Bishop Wilson had many high qualifications for his office. His episcopate was marked by the performance of a vast amount of work. His writings, his preaching, and his example, had a most beneficial effect on the inhabitants of Man. Many young men under his auspices started forth to fill the ministrations of this diocese. "With the pride and avarice of prelacy," says Robertson, "he was totally unacquainted. His palace was a temple of charity. Hospitality stood at his gate, and invited the stranger and beggar to a plenteous repast. The day he devoted to benevolence, and the night to piety."

He died on the 7th of March, 1755, in the 93rd year of his age, and the 58th year of his consecration, and was attended to his last resting-place in Kirk Michael churchyard by nearly the whole population of the isle. "I hope to look into his works," said Dr. Johnson, "for other purposes than those of criticism, and after their perusal, not only to write, but to live better." Dr. Mark Hildesley was appointed to the see in 1755. With the assistance of his clergy, he completed the translation of the Scriptures into the Manx tongue. He was succeeded in 1773 by Dr. Richmond, who is said to have been only remarkable for his unbending haughtiness. Mr. Crook, a Wesleyan minister, visited Man in 1775 and 1776, and encountered much opposition. The clergy were commanded by the bishop to present all persons who held any place under the ecclesiastical authority who should be found attending the ministrations of unauthorised teachers, and to repel from the Lord's table every such teacher that should offer to be a partaker of the holy communion. By this mandate, it has been asserted, the rabble were encouraged to continue their outrages. But the Governor, John Wood, Esq., protected Mr. Crook, and refused to permit the bishop's order to be read in his own chapel. The Lieutenant-Governor introduced the Wesleyan minister into the Governor's chapel, where the clergyman ventured to administer to him the holy communion; and after this none dared to molest Mr. Crook, who preached to large congregations near the Governor's gate, "the Governor and his family sitting in a convenient room to hear." The Rev. John Wesley visited the isle in 1777, and preached to immense multitudes in the church-yards and market-places. (The Wesleyan and Primitive Methodists have now upwards of sixty chapels in the Isle of Man). Dr. George Mason was appointed to the bishopric in 1780. His successor was Dr. Crigan. In 1814 the Hon. George Murray, son of Lord George Murray, the second son of the third Duke of Athole, was constituted bishop. He became very unpopular by attempting to commute the tithes for a fixed annual revenue of £6000, and when that project failed, by striving to enforce the collection of a tithe of all the green crops. In 1827 he was translated to the see of Rochester. Dr. Ward was the next bishop. This prelate, by appealing to his friends in England and the Isle of Man, succeeded in raising upwards of £12,000, which sum was expended in erecting eight new churches. He subscribed £1200 to the fund for building King William's College. In 1837 the see of Sodor and Man was annexed to that of Carlisle; but, in the following year, government was prevailed upon by the petitions of the inhabitants and of many influential persons in England, to restore the bishopric. The legislature passed an Act in 1839 to commute the tithes of the isle for £5050, which sum is thus apportioned:—£1505 to the lord bishop; £707 to the archdeacon; £303 each to the rectors of Ballaugh and Bride; £141 8s. each to the vicars of Arbory, Braddan, Conchan, German, Jurby, Lezayre, Lonan, Malew, Maughold, Marown, Michael, Patrick, Rushen, Santon, and to the trustees nominated in conveyance of the impropriate tithes of Michael, made by Bishop Wilson for the benefit of clergymen's widows; £101 to the chaplain of a chapel of ease in Andreas. These amounts are independent of the lands attached to the bishopric and the glebes attached to the vicarages. In 1840, to the great regret of the inhabitants, bishop Bowstead was translated to the see of Lichfield, and was succeeded by Dr. Pepys, who was soon after appointed to the see of Worcester. The next bishop was Dr. Short, who was consecrated in 1841. His successor was Dr. Shirley. In 1847 the Right Rev. Robert John Eden,

D.D., youngest son of the first Baron Auckland, was constituted bishop. He succeeded his brother in the peerages in 1849, and was translated in 1854 to the see of Bath and Wells. The Hon. and Right Rev. Horatio Powys, third son of the second Lord Lilford, was appointed to the bishopric in 1854. His lordship's ancestors were kings of Man in the ninth century.

The ancient armorial bearing of the see of Sodor and Man is, Azure, St. Columba at sea in a cock-boat, all proper, in chief, a blazing star, or. The present arms of the see are, on three ascents, the Virgin Mary, her arms extended between two pillars; on the dexter a church; in base the present arms of the island; ground an ornamental shield, surmounted by a bishop's mitre. The island having been a subordinate feudatory kingdom, the bishop of Sodor and Man, who is allowed a seat by courtesy in the House of Lords, has never had a voice in Parliament. Lord Auckland, as a peer of the realm, possessed the right of voting in the House of Lords.

CHAPTER IV.

CONSTITUTION, GOVERNMENT, ETC.

"The laws of a nation form the most instructive portion of its history."—GIBBON.

"THE Isle of Man," says Blackstone, "is a distinct territory from England, and is not governed by our laws: neither doth an Act of Parliament extend to it unless it be particularly named therein." This Liliputian kingdom does not form part of the realm of England; but it is part of the dominions of the Crown. It is not a foreign dominion, though it has its own legislature, laws, and courts of justice; and therefore a writ of *habeas corpus* can be issued to the Isle of Man. Its government is composed of the Queen in Council, the Lieutenant-Governor in Council, and the House of Keys. Laws of the insular legislature are only binding when they are passed with the consent of these three estates. The principal courts of law are, the Chancery, the General Gaol Delivery, the Exchequer, the Common Law, the Seneschal's, the Consistorial, and the High Bailiffs'. The twenty-four Keys, the Staff of Government, and lastly, the Queen in Council, possess appellate jurisdiction. For judicial purposes, the island is divided into two districts—the northern and southern—with a deemster* or judge, appointed by the Crown, for each. These districts are sub-divided

---

* "In the Isle of Man a proverbial expression forcibly indicates the object constantly occupying the minds of the inhabitants. The two deemsters or judges, when appointed to the chair of judgment, declare they will render justice between man and man 'as equally as the herring bone lies between the two sides:' an image which could not have occurred to any people unaccustomed to the herring fishery." — Disraeli's "Curiosities of Literature."

into sheadings, over each of which a coroner—an officer uniting in his person the duties of a constable and most of those of a sheriff in England—is appointed annually. The council consists of eight gentlemen, who hold their seats *ex officio*, namely, the Lord Bishop, the Archdeacon, the two Deemsters, the Attorney-General, the Clerk of the Rolls, the Vicar-General, and the Water-Bailiff. These gentlemen are appointed by the Crown. The Governor and Council form the upper branch of the Tynwald Court. The lower branch is the House of Keys. The Keys or Taxiaxi appear to have been elected in ancient times by the people. According to the old statute-book, under date 1422, they were twenty-four freeholders, to wit, eight in the out-isles, and sixteen in Man. At the present time, when a vacancy is occasioned by resignation or death, the majority of the remaining twenty-three elect two gentlemen of property, either of whom they deem eligible to occupy the vacant place. Their names are presented to the Lieutenant-Governor, who thereupon makes choice of one. The functions of the Keys when acting judicially, are very extensive. When sitting in their legislative capacity it is the duty of these gentlemen to propose such laws as may be thought conducive to the welfare of the isle, and send the same to the Lieutenant-Governor and Council for their consideration; and in like manner to receive from the Lieutenant-Governor and Council such bills as they may propose, and to consider, reject, amend, or approve the same. There appear to have been no written laws in Man prior to 1417, in which year Sir John Stanley visited the island for the purpose of causing the unwritten or "breast" laws —of which the deemsters were the sole depositaries and expounders—to be promulgated. They were then committed to writing, and formed the first statute-book of the isle. The insular judges, how-

ever, continued to administer "breast-law" justice
down to 1636, in which year they were ordered by
Lord Strange "to set down in writing and certify
...what these breast laws are;" and since that time
the legal decisions of the deemsters have been care-
fully recorded, and thus a valuable collection of
precedents has been formed for the guidance of those
who exercise judicial power in Man.

CHAPTER V.

NATURAL HISTORY: GEOLOGY, ZOOLOGY, AND BOTANY.

"The facts disclosed by geological investigation tend to
enlarge our conceptions of the attributes of the Divinity, and
of the sublimity of His plans and arrangements in the universe;
and to demonstrate that His creating power has been repeatedly
exercised during countless ages, in calling into existence
numerous orders of beings, and in carrying forward His
arrangements to a glorious consummation."—Dr. DICK.

GEOLOGY.

A BRIEF account of the geology of the Isle of Man
will not prove unacceptable to the reader. Professor
Forbes states that this isle is "mainly composed of
slate—both clay slate and mica slate—resting probably on granite. That rock makes its appearance
at the surface on a hill between Ramsey and Laxey
[at the Dhoon river], and protrudes through the
schist in an immense mass near Foxdale. The mountains are chiefly mica slate, which rock, at Greeba,
contains garnets. Quartz abounds both in the forms
of veins and detached masses, and in some places the
mica is found in fine silvery plates. In beds in the
clay slate, flinty slate and lydian stone are occa-

sionally found; and roofing slate is met with near Peel. At Spanish Head is a remarkable form of clay slate, much used as lintels and door-posts, and which is slightly flexible in thin masses. On the coast, the clay slate passes into grey-wacke-slate, and that rock into grey-wacke. At Kirk Santon Head, the conglomerated structure of the grey-wacke-rock is finely developed. . .The lead and copper mines of Foxdale, Laxey, and Brada, are all in the slate rocks.* The lead ores are very rich in silver. The other rocks of the island are sandstone and limestone. The sandstone is that ancient secondary rock termed old red sandstone, and is found at Peel resting on the slate. Of this sandstone Peel Castle is built. . .The limestone is that kind known to geologists as the carboniferous or mountain limestone, and more recently termed by Professor Phillips, the lower scar limestone, and which, in the coal formations of England, lies immediately beneath that valuable bituminous mineral. At Poolvash [where the stone forming the steps which ascend to the entrance of St. Paul's Cathedral was obtained] it abounds with fossil shells. The genera *Producta, Spirifera, Terebratula, Goniatites, Nautilus,* and *Orthoceras* are exceedingly numerous, while the *Sanguinolaria, Cypricardia, Pinna, Inoceramus, Avicula, Gervilia,* and *Pecten* occur more rarely. The crustaceous remains are so exceedingly rare that the *Asaphus quadrilimbus* and *A. seminiferus* are only recognised by some mutilated fragments. . .In the neighbourhood of Castletown, the limestone rests on grey-wacke. It is of a very hard and firm texture,

---

* "It sometimes happens that schists and slates are associated with large quantities of siliceous matter, forming a very hard but irregular mass; and when exposed to the action of the sea, this decomposes in a striking manner, producing very bold sea cliffs. This is the case on the coasts of the Isle of Man, where Douglas Harbour shows very beautifully the form which such rock can assume."—Orr's "Circle of the Sciences."

and much used for public works. Castle Rushen and the College are built of it. . .Between Poolvash and Scarlett some interesting appearances present themselves. Veins of trap, from two to six feet in breadth, appear breaking through the limestone, showing evident proof of their former fused state; these veins generally assume the amygdaloidal form, sometimes that of greenstone. Scattered through the mass appear broken fragments of the limestone, having a flinty hardness; and for some feet from the junction, all traces of organic life are obliterated. Through the trap sometimes runs veins of quartz, in various directions, hollow in the middle, and crystallised in prisms, which generally meet, but when terminated, end with their edges bevelled. In several places, both in the limestone and slate, specimens of anthracite, or blind coal, occur, which has been often mistaken by the inhabitants for bituminous coal, and led to many useless researches for that mineral. The north of the island is nearly a flat plain of sand and peat-bogs. The peat rests on beds of clay-marl, which includes strata of gravel and sea sand, containing shells belonging to the present era, bleached, but often tolerably perfect. The most frequent species are *Tellina solidula, Venus cassina, Astarte scotica,* and *Turitella terebra,* all of them existing at present in the neighbouring sea. This marl also envelopes the osseous remains of *Cervus megaceros,* or great fossil elk." A splendid specimen of this extinct animal was discovered at Ballacain many years ago. It may be seen in the museum of the University of Edinburgh. It is six feet in height, and nine in length: its height to the tip of the right antler is nine feet seven inches and a half. Professor Owen says:—"The formerly unique skeleton of the megaceros in the museum of the University of Edinburgh was obtained from a formation in the Isle of Man, which Mr. E. Forbes,

Professor of Botany in King's College, London, informs me is a white marl, with freshwater shells found in detached masses, occupying hollows in the red marl; which red marl, by the proportion of marine shells of the species found in the neighbouring seas, is referable to the newer pliocene period. The cervine fossils have never been met with in the marine or red marls in the Isle of Man, but only in the white marls occupying the freshwater basins of the red marl; and from the position of the beds containing the remains of the megaceros, Professor Forbes concludes that this gigantic species must have

existed posterior to the elevation of the newer pliocene marl, which is probably continuous with the same formation in Lancashire and at the mouth of the Clyde, forming a great plain, extending from Scotland to Cheshire, and now for the most part covered by the sea. The geographical features of the dry land, the seat of those lakes in which the remains of the megaceros are most commonly found, would seem, therefore, to have undergone much change since the time of its extinction."

ZOOLOGY.

Of the zoology of the island we can undertake to give but a limited account. Giraldus asserts that a dispute once took place between the kings of England and Ireland for this little domain, and it was agreed to be amicably settled by the introduction, from England, of venemous reptiles, which would not live in *Ireland.* The reptiles *lived;* and consequently the King of England took possession of the isle. At the present, time, however, according to the distinguished Manx naturalist from whose work we have made copious extracts, the island "is exempt from venemous reptiles and toads; but frogs are abundant, though they are popularly believed to have been imported—an idea for which there is no foundation. *Lacerta sterpium,* sand lizard, is common in the north; *L. Agilis,* common lizard, abounds in old hedges and dry banks in every part of the island. *Triton palustris,* warty eft, and *T. punctatus,* common eft, are by no means rare. . .It is said that deer formerly inhabited the mountains; but they, like their great prototype, the fossil elk, have long since passed away. The only remarkable quadruped peculiar to the island is the tailless cat, an accidental variety of the common species, *Felis catus,* frequently showing no traces of caudal vertebra, and in others a merely rudimental substitute for it." Wood, in his "Natural History," states that these cats are of the Chartreuse breed. Train says that they resemble somewhat in appearance the cats said by Sir S. Raffles to be peculiar to the Malayan Archipelago. A writer in *Once a Week* (Dec. 26, 1863) asserts that "the tailless Manx cats approach the wild cat very nearly in ferocity and appearance." The representation of a tailless cat, crouching on the croup of a horse, may be seen on the inner wall of an Etruscan tomb (see *The Athenæum,* Jan. 13, 1849).

"Of game birds, a few of the partridge and quail remain, but grouse is no longer to be found. Snipes are abundant. That rare bird, the Manx puffin, *Procellaria anglorum*, formerly an inhabitant of the Calf, is no longer to be found there. The red-legged crow is common; the king-fisher scarce; and the hoopoe, the goatsucker, the shrike, the cross-bill, and the roller have been killed on the island.

Many rare fishes are found in the neighbouring sea. The *Squatina angelus*, or angel-fish; the *Lophius piscatorius*, or fishing frog; and the *Spinachia vulgaris*, or sea stickle-back, are by no means uncommon. In the markets may be found *Trigla Hirundo*, *pini*, *lineatus*, and *gurnardus*, and *Pagrus vulgaris*. In the harbour and on the coasts, the *Pholis lævus; Merlangus virens; Crenilabrus tinca; Labrus lineatus*, *maculatus*, and *pusillus; Trachinus draco* and *vipera: Gunnellus vulgaris* and *Ammodytes lancea* and *tobianus* abound. Occasionally may be found with them the *Gobius minutus*, and *Sygnathus ophidion*, *æquoreus*, and *acus*, &c."

BOTANY.

According to Professor Forbes, the Isle of Man is not remarkably rich in plants. It contains about five hundred species of the flowering kinds. A list of the more rare, indicating the localities where they may be found, is subjoined:—

Sparganium simplex (bur-reed). Ditches in Curraghs.
Scirpus Savii. Douglas Bay and Derbyhaven.
Juncus maritimus. Scarlett.
Alisma ranunculoides (lesser water-plantain). Curraghs.
Scilla verna. Douglas Head, and other cliffs by the sea.
Polygonum Raii. Derbyhaven and Ballaugh.
Anagallis tenella (pimpernel). Bogs.
Pinguicula lusitanica. Boggy spots near Derby Castle.
Euphrasia (eyebright). Fields by the sea at Ballaugh.
Verbascum Thapsus (great mullein). Near Miltown.
Hyoscyamus niger (black henbane). Poolvash, Derbyhaven.
Solanum nigrum (black nightshade). Near Snaefell.

Lycopus Europæus (water horehound). Curraghs.
Pulegium vulgare (pennyroyal). Marl pits at Ballaugh.
Stachys ambigua (woundwort). North of the island.
Lamium intermedium. Kirk Michael, &c.
Lamium amplexicaule. With the last.
Scutellaria minor. (lesser skull-cap). Onchan, &c.
Convolvulus Soldanella (sea-bindweed). Point of Ayre,
     Ballaugh, &c.
Erythræa latifolia. Cliffs by the sea.
Carduus marianus (milk-thistle). Sandy fields at Ballaugh.
Carduus tenuifloris. Common.
Bidens tripartita. Northern districts.
Artemisia maritima (sea-wormwood). Near Snaefell.
Gnaphalium margaritacum. Hedges near Ballachurry, Andreas.
Pyrethrum maritimum. Cliffs by the sea.
Helioscidium nodiflorum. Ditches in Jurby.
Crethmum maritimum (sea-samphire). Cliffs at St. Anne's
     Head.
Eryngium maritimum. North coast, &c.
Erodium maritimum (sea-stork's bill). Castletown.
Geranium pusillum. (Small flowered crane's-bill). Scarlett.
Lavatera arborea (tree mallow). Near Spanish Head, &c.
Malva moschata. Sea cliffs and roadsides.
Linum angustifolium. Field beyond Derby Castle.
Radiolus millegranus. Wet places.
Orobanche major (common broom-rape). Lezayre.
Listera ovata (common twayblade). Castletown.
Hypericum elodes. Bogs.
Hypericum androsæmum. Port Soderick.
Crambe maritima (sea kale). Near Peel.
Thlaspi arvense (shepherd's-purse). Sandy fields.
Lepidium campestre. Common.
Lepidium Smithii. Ballaugh.
Cochlearia Grænlandica. Cliffs near Peel.
Erysimum cheiranthoides. Roadsides at Ballaugh.
Brassica Monensis. Grounds at Castle Mona, Andreas, &c.
Resida fructiculosa. On a wall at Ballaugh Rectory.
Viola montana. North of the island.
Viola Curtisii. Near the sea, Michael.
Silene Anglica (common English campion). Jurby.
Cerastium tetrandrum. Sandy fields in northern districts.
Cerastium arvense. Derbyhaven.
Spergula maritimum. Ramsey, and Peel Castle.
Sedum Anglicum. On rocks and old walls.
Cotyledon umbilicus (navelwort). On walls everywhere.
Tormentilla reptans. Hedges.

Rubus saxatilis. Glen at Bishop's Court.
Ulex nanus (dwarf furze). On heaths and hedges.
Vicia angustifolia. Sandy fields, Andreas.
Vicia lathyroides. With the last.
Ornithopus perpusillus (bird's-foot). Sandy fields.
Trifolium fragiferum. Ballaugh.
Euphorbia Portlandica. Walbury.
Asplenium marinum (sea fern). On rocks by the sea.
Osmunda regalis (flowering fern). Andreas, on the Calf, &c.
Adiantum capillus veneris. Glen Meay, Ruins of St. Trinion's, &c.

CHAPTER VI.

ANTIQUITIES.

" "Time, which antiquates antiquities, and hath an art to make
dust of all things, hath yet spared these ... monuments."—
SIR THOMAS BROWNE.

WE believe that the following brief account of some
of the most remarkable antiquities of the Isle of
Man will not prove entirely devoid of interest. They
consist of—

BARROWS, or mounds of earth raised over the remains of the dead. Monuments of this kind abound
in the island. Of these the most notable are Cronk-
ny-Marroo, *i.e.*, Hill of the Dead, near Greenwick in
the parish of Santon; Cronk Aust, near Ramsey;
Cronk-y-Vowlan, in Bride; and Cronk-Ballavarry,
and Cronk-y-Dooney, in Andreas. Others may be
seen near Tynwald Hill, on Lambfell, and on the
mountains of Archallagan. Worsaae remarks:—
"They are met with mostly on hills and near the
firths or sea-coasts, whence there is an uninterrupted
view of the sea. To the ancient Northman it was
evidently an almost insufferable thought to be buried

in a confined or remote corner, where nobody could
see his grave or be reminded of his deeds.   The
greater chief a man was, the more did he desire that
his barrow should lie high and unenclosed, so that it
might be visible to all who travelled by land and by
sea."   Many sepulchral tumuli, full of burnt bones,
may be seen near Bishop's Court.

BAUTA STONES (*bautasteinar*), tall, slender stones,
placed in an upright position, and standing two or
three yards out of the ground.   These rude monumental stones were erected by the Scandinavians in
memory of their most distinguished warriors.   "As
to funeral rites," says Snorre Sturlason, "the earliest
age is called the Age of Burning; because all the
dead were consumed by fire, and over their ashes
were raised bauta stones."   A mutilated bauta stone
may be seen near Mount Murray.   According to
Olaus Magnus, larger monumental stones were also
erected by the Northmen.   Speaking of the stone-
groupings of Norway, he remarks: "These stones
raised in many places, are from ten to thirty feet
high, notably situated, and placed in wonderful
order with some notable character.   They signify,
when of right long order, the battles of champions:
by a square order, troops of warriors: by a round
order, the burials of families: and by a wedge form,
they show that near that place an army of foot and
horse had fortunately prevailed."   In the Isle of
Man, the Giant's Quoiting Stones and the Cloven
stones, &c., are undoubtedly Scandinavian monuments.

ANCIENT BURIAL-PLACES, which are frequently discovered by farmers in ploughing their fields.   Sometimes many stone coffins, in which the remains of the
dead have been placed, are found side by side.
Occasionally a kist-vaen is found to contain cinerary
urns.

CAIRNS (*Dysser*), Scandinavian burial-places, formed

of a heap of stones thrown together, and not covered with earth. One of these, in a dilapidated state, stands on the hill north-east of Laxey. A kist-vaen was found in it.

CASTLES. These may be seen at Castletown and Peel, and are described in Chapters VIII. and X. of this work.

COINS. Many ancient coins have been discovered, among which may be mentioned coins of Germanicus and Agrippina, found at Castletown (?); of the Anglo-Saxon king Ethelred the Unready, found at Bradhawe; of the celebrated Canute, found at Castletown; of Henry II., found at Balladoole; of Edward I., found in Marown; and of Edward III., found on Douglas Head and at Slegaby in Onchan. In Waldron's "Description" of Man, there are engravings of several curious tokens which, he states, were discovered in the island.

STONE CIRCLES, which zealous antiquaries have erroneously classed amongst Druidical remains. It has been ascertained beyond doubt that they are of Scandinavian origin. "These stone circles," says Worsaae, "belong simply to low graves encircled by stones, like those so frequently found in Norway, and whose date is of the latest period of heathenism, or what is called the iron age." One of the largest of these is at Glen Darragh. On the estate of Ballakelly, in Santon, on Mount Karran, and on Spanish Head (near the Chasms), smaller stone circles stand. There are more than twenty of these circular inclosures on the island.

FORTIFICATIONS. Derby Fort, built of stone, is on St. Michael's islet. See Chapter VIII. An ancient fort, of which a view is given in Chapter VII., formerly stood on the Pollock Rock in Douglas Bay. Others (of earth) may be seen near Kirk Christ, Rushen; at Balla Nicholas, in Marown; at Ferk, in Santon; at Castleward, in Braddan; at Corvalley, in

German; and at Ballachurry, in Andreas. The ruins
of a remarkable old encampment stand in the vicinity
of Kirk Braddan.

RUNIC REMAINS, consisting of monumental crosses.
The isle abounds with these interesting memorials of
the past. "The Norwegian monuments in the Isle
of Man," says Worsaae, "are in themselves numerous and considerable enough to convey an idea of the
power which the Norwegians must have possessed
there." Many of these ancient crosses are remarkable for the beautiful artistic designs which ornament
them. They are decorated with reticulated and geo-
metrical tracery, with representations of serpents,
dragons, and various fanciful animals—evidently borrowed from the northern mythology, — and with
figures of men, horses, dogs, stags, and birds. On
many of these relics of the Scandinavians are Runic
inscriptions* in the Old Norse tongue. An inscrip-

---

* "The art of writing," says Rask, "was already known in
the North long before the introduction of Christianity; the
characters then in use are called Runes (rún, plural runir, old
runar)...Our forefathers kept far into the Christian times the
old characters, in inscriptions on gravestones, staves, and calen-
dars, for which they were far more fit than the Roman letters.
Of the Runic orthography it is especially to be remarked, that
in the oldest period it never doubled any letter; that the words
were commonly separated by one, sometimes two points; that
the arrangement of the lines was irregular, and must be found
out by the context; that the runic characters were often
written reversely from right to left; and that some letters, in
remote places and in different times, seem to have had different
meanings, which is especially the case with the vowels, though
here a difference of dialect may have had some influence. The
antiquity of Runes has indeed been denied by many learned
men, but yet seems thoroughly credible, for the following rea-
sons. At the introduction of Christianity and for some time
after, they were in general use over the whole North, in Sweden,
Denmark, Norway, and Iceland, and we have demonstrably
heathen Runic stones, on which Thor is invoked...That they
were sometimes used of old in sorcery is rather a reason for, than
an objection against their high antiquity. All writers assign

tion on a cross at Kirk Michael states that these
admirable specimens of ancient art were the workmanship of one Gaut: "Gaut made this [cross] and
all on Man." Others state that "these runes" were
engraved by Ina the Swarthy and by Thurid. Pro-
fessors Munch and Worsaae are of opinion that these
inscriptions were for the most part engraved in the
eleventh century. The annexed wood-cut (p. 78)
exhibits all the Runic inscriptions in the Isle of Man,
with the exception of that on Ofeig's cross at Kirk
Braddan.

---

with one voice their introduction into the North to Odin. . .
The Runes have great likeness to the oldest Greek alphabet,
and this coincides completely with the old story of our forefathers having flitted hither from the country north of the
Black Sea."

In his Origin and Progress of Writing, Astle remarks : "Our
opinion on the evidence before us is, that the Runic characters
are composed partly of ancient Gothic and Greek letters, and
partly of Roman, deformed and corrupted, probably by the
necromancers of the North, who used them in spells and incan-
tations. In 1001 the Swedes were persuaded by the Pope to
lay aside the Runic letters, and to adopt the Roman in their
room. In 1115 the Runic letters were condemned in Spain by
the Council of Toledo. They were abolished in Denmark in the
beginning of the fourteenth century, and in Iceland soon after."

In Chapter IX. of the Decline and Fall of the Roman Empire,
Gibbon observes : "We may rest contented with this decisive
authority," [namely, the words of Tacitus : *Literarum secreta
viri pariter ac fœminæ ignorant*,] "without entering into the ob-
scure disputes concerning the antiquity of the Runic characters.
The learned Celsius, a Swede, a scholar, and a philosopher, was
of opinion that they were nothing more than the Roman letters
with the curves turned into straight lines for the ease of engraving. . .We may add that the oldest Runic inscriptions are
supposed to be of the third century, and the most ancient writer
who mentions the Runic characters is Venantius Fortunatus
(Camm. vii., 18), who lived towards the end of the sixth century.

'Barbara fraxineis pingatur Runa tabellis.' "

"There is no longer any doubt," says Carl Lottner, "that
the Runes are derived from the Roman uncials."—See *Fraser's
Magazine, August, 1861.*

	Nº 1	Nº 2
F...	ᚠ	ᚠ
U,V,Y(o)	ᚢ	ᚢ
Đ,Th.	ᚦ	ᚦ
O,A,	ᚨ	ᚼ
R...	ᚱ	ᚱ
K,G.	ᚴ	ᚴ
H...		ᚼ
N...	ᚾ	ᚾ
I,J(e)	ᛁ	ᛁ
A...	ᛁᛏ	ᛁᛏ
E...	ᚼᛏ	ᛏᚼ
S...	ᛌᚾ	ᛌᚢ
T,D.	ᛁᛏ	ᛁᛏ
B,P.	ᛒ	ᛒ
L...	ᛚ	ᛚ
M...	ᛘ	ᛘ
Y,R.		ᛉ

Difference of opinion prevails as to the etymology of the woid Rune. Some assert that it is derived from *Ryn*, a furrow or channel (Olaus Wormius, "Literatura Runica," p. 2). Others consider it to have been taken from the Teutonic word *Runa*, which signifies mystery. Runic letters have been divided into three classes, the Scandinavian, the German, and the Anglo - Saxon. The German Runic characters are supposed by Grimm to be a late modification of the Scandinavian runes, as the Anglo-Saxon are of the German. In the "Nouveau Traité de Diplomatique," (1750), t. i., p. 713, is a plate representing every possible Runic character, there being as many as from fifteen to forty-one different shapes given for each letter. The authors (Deux Religieux Bénédictins de la Congrégation de S. Maur) say : "On sera sans doute éffrayé de leur multitude, mais on sera rassuré quand on saura que nul monument, nul MS., nul ouvrage, ne les réunit tous, ni même un grand nombre d'entr'eux." In the preceding engraving (p. 79) we give the Manx (No. 1) and the Scandinavian (No. 2) Runic alphabets.

ROUND TOWERS. One of these singular towers may be seen at Peel Castle. Ireland abounds with these ancient structures, which are supposed by Dr. Petrie to be ecclesiastical edifices, ranging in date from the introduction of Christianity into that country down to the tenth century. He maintains that they were not only designed for belfries and watch-towers, but for strongholds whither the clergy could retreat with their most valuable effects when threatened with danger from the assaults of barbarian spoilers.

ECCLESIASTICAL ANTIQUITIES. Of these, the following are deserving of remark:—The ruins of Rushen Abbey, at Ballasalla; of the Cathedral of St. German, and St. Patrick's Church in Peel Castle; Of St. Trinion's Church in Marown; of St. Bridget's Nunnery, at Douglas; and of the Friary of Bimakin or Brymaken, in Arbory. The Treen Chapels, all of which are much dilapidated, are worthy of special notice. According to an old Manx ballad, they were erected by St. German. Treen Chapels may be seen at Camlork and Mount Rule, in Braddan; at Ballafreer, Ballingan, Ballalough, Ballaquinney-mooar, Rhyne, and Ballachrink, in Marown; at Balladoole, in Arbory; and at West Nappin, in Jurby.

TYNWALD HILL, an artificial mount, from which all Manx laws are promulgated. See Chapter X.

MISCELLANEOUS ANTIQUITIES. Amongst these may be specified rings and bracelets; querns or handmills; weapons of bronze and iron, including swords, daggers, celts, and gauntlets; and other objects too numerous to mention in this brief sketch.

CHAPTER VII.

DESCRIPTION OF DOUGLAS, AND THE PARISHES OF BRAD-
DAN, ONCHAN, LONAN, MAROWN, AND SANTON.

"Fair scenes for childhood's opening bloom;
For sportive youth to play in;
For manhood to enjoy his strength;
And age to wear away in!"

WORDSWORTH.

DOUGLAS, the largest town in the Isle of Man, and by
far the most important emporium for commerce, is
situated in a magnificent crescent-shaped bay, bounded
on the north and south by bold and rocky headlands.
The town derives its name from the junction of two
streams—the Doo (black) and Glass (gray, or clear)—
which disembogue themselves into the sea at this
place. Its aspect from the sea is singularly beautiful.
The elegant villas, terraces of houses, and castellated
mansions, clustered round the capacious and enchanting bay, make a most agreeable impression upon the
eye; and the mountains, at a distance of seven or eight
miles, form a noble background. It is generally
admitted that as a bathing-place this picturesque and
extensive bay—around the entire margin of which
the waves have laid a carpet of the smoothest sand—
is unsurpassed. Strangers are immediately struck
with the marvellous transparency of the water.

The town bears a high character for salubrity.
The air is wholesome and temperate, neither too hot
in summer, nor too cold in winter, and the successive
seasons fall so insensibly into one another, that the
transition is scarcely felt by the most delicate constitution. Douglas, which at the beginning of the
eighteenth century was a mere fishing-village, is now
a place of considerable importance. It is rapidly
assuming a modern aspect, the houses are gradually
beautifying, and the streets extending themselves. The
town will soon possess all the usual attractions of a
fashionable watering-place. The population in 1861

was 12,389.   A picturesque edifice, styled the Tower
of Refuge, stands on St. Mary's Rock, or Conister, in
Douglas Bay.   It was erected in 1832 for the safety
of shipwrecked mariners, by the late Sir W. Hillary,
Bart., who, during his residence at Douglas, founded
the Royal National Life-Boat Institution.   In the
night, this tower has the appearance of a square-
rigged sloop under sail.

Occasionally in winter,

"The startled waves leap over it ; the storm
Smites it with all the scourges of the rain,
And steadily against its solid form
Press the great shoulders of the hurricane."

Wordsworth, who visited the Isle of Man in 1833,
thus alludes to this building and its philanthropic
founder :

"The feudal keep, the bastions of Cohorn,
Even when they rose to check or to repel
Tides of aggressive war, oft served as well
Greedy ambition, armed to treat with scorn

Just limits; but yon tower, whose smiles adorn
This perilous bay, stands clear of all offence;
Blest work it is of love and innocence,
A tower of refuge to the else forlorn.
Spare it, ye waves, and lift the mariner,
Struggling for life, into its saving arms!
Spare, too, the human helpers ! Do they stir
'Mid your fierce shock like men afraid to die ?
No, their dread service nerves the heart it warms,
And they are led by noble Hillary."

Douglas possesses an extensive pier—a favourite promenade of the inhabitants,—and a capacious and secure harbour. The first stone of the pier was laid on the 24th of July, 1793, by John, Duke of Athole : on the eastern extremity of this structure stands a small lighthouse. In 1837 a jetty was erected on the south side of the harbour. Douglas harbour admits vessels of considerable burden, the depth of the water at spring tides being nearly twenty feet. On the western extremity of the pier stands the Imperial Hotel, an elegant and spacious edifice recently erected by Samuel Harris, Esq., the worthy High Bailiff of Douglas. The apartments are splendid, and furnished with an unsurpassable luxury. This hotel is charmingly situated, and commands a noble prospect. The Watch-House, where a record is kept of all vessels entering and leaving the port, is also on the pier.

From this admirable marine promenade, Douglas Head, which forms the southern boundary of the bay, may be surveyed. The principal lighthouse stands on its eastern extremity: the light, which is stationary, is visible in clear weather at a distance of fourteen miles. The adjacent creek, called Port Skillion, is greatly resorted to by bathers. A little to the westward is an old fortification—erected during the panic excited by Napoleon Bonaparte's threatened invasion—in the immediate vicinity of which are two newly-constructed batteries mounting heavy guns. From a rocky point beneath these defensive works, the Breakwater—an unfinished wooden structure, of considerable length—juts out into the blue waters of the bay. Three years ago the Commissioners. of Harbours informed the Lords of the Treasury that "the mode of construction of the proposed works has been the subject of much public discussion, and doubts as to their durability, more especially in very deep water and in an exposed situation such as Douglas Bay, very extensively prevail." The works, however, were commenced in the spring of 1862; and large sums of money were expended in erecting this flimsy structure, a considerable portion of which was swept away by the winds and waves on the 29th of January, 1865. It is highly probable that the breakwater now in process of construction will be shortly cased with stone.

Harold Tower and Ravenscliffe next attract attention. In the former mansion, the residence of Mrs. Wilson, a relative of the celebrated Martin, are many of the finest paintings of that distinguished artist.* Amongst these may be specified Christ stilling the Storm on the Lake of Genesereth; Elijah ascending to Heaven in a Chariot (water-colour); a Scene from Byron's "Heaven and Earth" (water-colour); Scottish Lake and Mountain Scenery, illustrative of a scene from Miss Porter's novel, "The Scottish Chiefs" (water-colour); and The Meeting of Jacob and Esau

---

* "But I hasten to Martin—the greatest, the most lofty, the most permanent, the most original genius of his age. I see in him. . .the presence of a spirit which is not of the world—the divine intoxication of a great soul lapped in majestic and unearthly dreams. . .Vastness is his sphere—yet he has not lost or circumfused his genius in its space; he has chained, and wielded it, and measured it, at his will; he has transfused its character into narrow limits; he has compassed the Infinite itself with a mathematical precision. He is not, it is true, a Raffaelle, delineating and varying human passion, or arresting the sympathy of passion itself in a profound and sacred calm; he is not a Michael Angelo, the creator of gigantic and preternatural powers—the Titans of the ideal heaven. But he is more original, more self-dependent than either: they perfected the style of others;. . .Martin has borrowed from none."—BULWER.

in the Wilderness. Martin was engaged in finishing
this oil-painting when he was seized with paralysis.
In Harold Tower there are also valuable paintings
by Mrs. Wilson's son-in-law, E. C. Corbould, Esq.,
and by —— Warren, Esq.

Fort Anne Hotel—a great ornament to the headland on which it stands—next attracts the eye. It
was formerly the residence of the eccentric Thomas
Whaley, and of Sir W. Hillary, Bart. Adjacent to
this handsome edifice are a castellated building, a
terrace of excellent dwelling-houses designated Fort-
William, and Taubman-terrace.

Leaving the pier, and proceeding westward, we
pass by the Reading-room of the United Service
Club, the Sailors' Home, and the premises of the
Steam Packet Company, beyond which is that attractive and commodious building, the Royal Hotel.
The Market-place next claims attention. On its
north side stands the chapel-of-ease dedicated to St.
Matthew, an unpretending structure, erected in 1708
by Bishop Wilson; on its west side is the "British,"
an excellent and spacious hotel. Entering *Duke-
street*, a street of handsome and commodious shops,
a few paces bring us to *Lord-street* (branching to the
left), in which was born the late Professor Forbes, of
the University of Edinburgh. The next opening is
King-street, in which is the office of the *Manx Sun*,
a weekly newspaper. Proceeding further up Duke-
street, we pass by an opening called *Wellington-
buildings*, where the insular newspaper entitled *Mona's
Herald* is printed. The next turning on the west side
is *Wellington-street*, in which stand the Primitive-
Methodist Chapel and the Theatre. In *Thomas-street*,
which extends from Wellington-street to King-street,
is a spacious chapel belonging to the Wesleyan-
Methodists.

Retracing our steps to Duke-street, the lofty and
commodious building styled the *Wellington Market*
attracts the eye: the large room over this market is

used for concerts and public meetings. The second
opening, on the east side of the street, is called *Fort-
street*,.   It is indebted for its name to a circular
castellated fort which formerly stood near its eastern
termination on the bight of the Pollock Rock, the
original entrance to the harbour of Douglas.   This
ancient structure, which is represented in the annexed
wood-cut, was not without historical associations.

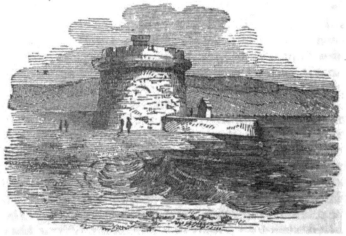

Two centuries ago it was occupied by a small armed
force, and possessed four pieces of cannon ; and four
of the inhabitants of Douglas kept watch and ward
on the rampart between the fort and town.   Its
demolition took place in 1818.   Adjacent to the site
of the fort are M'Ghie's Marine Baths, not far from
which (on the Parade) is the office of the *Isle of Man
Times*.   In Fort-street are the Hospital, the Town
Commissioners' Office, and the Church of St. Barna-
bas.   The latter edifice is in the early English style
of architecture, and was founded in 1830 by Bishop
Ward.   It contains fifteen hundred sittings, of which
five hundred are free : there is a neat tower at the
west end, surmounted by a lofty spire.   It may be here
remarked that in the adjacent residence of Richard
Quirk, Esq., Receiver-General—an intimate friend of

the late Professor Forbes—there is a splendid oil-painting (a portrait of a lady) by Sir Godfrey Kneller.

To Duke-street, *Strand-street* and *Castle-street* form a continuous line of road. At the north end of Castle-street is an exceedingly elegant church, in the

early English style of architecture, erected in 1850
from the design of Ewan Christian, Esq.   It is
dedicated to St. Thomas, possesses eight very musical
bells, and contains one thousand sittings, of which
five hundred are free.   It is to be regretted that,
owing to the inadequacy of the funds, the erection of
the spire, a conspicuous feature in the design, is in-
definitely postponed.   Contiguous to St. Thomas's
parsonage are Wallace's Marine Baths.

Retracing our steps to the Market-place, we proceed westward along the Quay.   The harbour extends
the whole length of the town from east to west.   The
last opening on the right hand communicates with
Athole-street, a genteel street, chiefly composed of
private houses.   St. James's Hall, which is used for
lectures and public meetings, presents itself on the
left-hand side : the meetings of the Manx Society for
the publication of documents relating to the history
of the isle are held in one of the rooms connected
with this hall.   On the right-hand side of the street
will be perceived the Lancasterian Schools.   The
principal edifice in Athole-street is the Court House,
a handsome structure erected in 1841.   Here may be
seen a marble bust of the late professor Forbes.

In this building, which is unquestionably one of the finest architectural ornaments of Douglas, the courts of law are held. Adjacent to the Court House, in *Church-street*, is the Adelphi Hotel, a commodious and well-conducted house. On the right-hand side of Athole-street is the Post-office, opposite to which stand the Independent Chapel and the premises of the Electric Telegraph Company. At the extremity of the street is St. George's Hall. *Prospect-hill* is now reached. On its east side is the Victoria Hotel, a handsome building occupying a commanding position. Adjacent to it is the Victoria Hall, a noble structure, which is used for lectures, concerts, and public meetings: the appearance of the interior is exceedingly attractive. The Bank of Mona, a very beautiful edifice, next presents itself. In the same street is the Bank of Messrs. Dumbell, Son, and Howard—a structure of much architectural merit. The new Roman Catholic Church, an elegant and majestic edifice, stands on the west side of Prospect-hill: its lofty towers rise above all the surrounding buildings. Diverging to the left we reach St. George's Church, which is surrounded by an extensive cemetery. This church was commenced in 1761 and finished in 1780, and will accommodate one thousand persons: the organ is of excellent quality. Proceeding up Prospect-hill, we reach *Buck's-road*, which contains many neat and commodious dwelling-houses. Several newly-erected streets branching from it communicate with Finch-road. Advancing northward, we come to the House of Industry, a substantial structure with a square tower, erected in 1837: it is supported by voluntary subscriptions. For this excellent institution the poor of the town are principally indebted to the exertions of the Rev. Dr. Carpenter. A short distance beyond, *Windsor-road* branches to the right. The first street on the left-

hand side of this road conducts to the Middle School,
a handsome stone structure in the Gothic style,
erected at the expense of Mrs. Cecil Hall: the course
of instruction is very comprehensive. We return to
Buck's-road, pursuing which, we pass by Adelaide,
Prospect, and Westview Terraces, and reach *Derby-road* or *Lover's-lane* (branching to the right), at the
corner of which stands Woodbourne-house. Entering Derby-road, *Derby-square* is soon reached: here
are many genteel residences. On arriving at the
extremity of the road, we come to Broadway, and,
turning to the right, approach the picturesque bay of
Douglas. Pursuing the road by the sea on the left,
we reach Clarence-terrace. At the end of this handsome terrace—which commands extensive and beautiful prospects—is Maxwell's Boarding-house. The
Esplanade, Derby-terrace, and Castle-terrace next
attract attention. Beyond these is that magnificent
edifice Castle Mona Hotel, the attractive *locale* of
which, in close proximity to the beach (on which
excellent and safe bathing may be enjoyed at all
hours of the tide), together with the splendour of its
appointments, its vast extent of accommodation, and
withal its apt illustration of the cosy and comfortable,
have rendered it a favourite temporary residence with
the nobility and gentry who resort during the summer
months to the Isle of Man. This superb edifice,
formerly the residence of John, Duke of Athole, is
built of freestone from the Isle of Arran, and is said
to have cost upwards of forty thousand pounds. It
is a square structure, with a wing on the south side,
and is surmounted by a circular embattled tower.
On the east front, which recedes a little in the centre,
may be seen the armorial bearings of the Athole
family. The principal entrance is under a lofty
portico on the south side. The building is represented in the annexed engraving.

As an exterior view affords but little information regarding the internal arrangements, it may be stated, in further elucidation of the structure, that on the ground floor there are a noble banqueting-room, a

grand saloon, and suites of elegant drawing-rooms.
The bed-rooms and dressing-rooms are in the upper
portion of the building. The prospects from the
windows are magnificent. The grounds are extensive
(about twenty acres being reserved for the use of
visitors), and the gardens are planted with great
taste. Contiguous, on an eminence called Falcon
Cliff, is a beautiful castellated edifice, which commands a glorious view of the bay and the surrounding scenery. Beyond are several detached villas and
many genteel residences. Advancing northward, we
reach Athole Academy, of which Dr. McBurney is the
principal. The course of study includes classics,
mathematics, and the various branches of a sound
English education. The Crescent Academy, of which
Dr. Steele is the principal, next attracts attention.
In this academy young gentlemen are efficiently prepared for the universities, the army, the navy, and
the learned professions, or to enter with credit on
mercantile pursuits. We now approach Strathallan
Crescent and Lodge. The adjacent edifice, called
Derby Castle, is one of the chief architectural orna-
ments of the beautiful locality in which it is situate.
Ascending Burntmill-hill, we come to Strathallan
Park, in which are numerous elegant mansions, com-
manding charming prospects of the bay and town of
Douglas.

Penetrating no further north, we retrace our steps
to Broadway, whence we proceed along the *Colonel's-
road*, on the right-hand side of which is the delightfully situated Villa Marina Hotel. It is concealed
from the road by a high stone wall. The pleasure-
grounds are beautifully laid out.

Thanks to Samuel Harris, Esq., the chief magistrate
of Douglas, a noble marine promenade, now in process
of construction, will soon extend along the margin of
the bay.

Beyond Villa Marina Hotel is Marina-terrace. The

fist opening on the right conducts to *Finch-road*, on the west side of which are several terraces of houses, occupying elevated positions and commanding splendid views. At No. 4 in Finch-road died Martin, the distinguished artist. At its southern extremity stands the Presbyterian Church, beyond which is Prospect-hill.

The environs of Douglas, which we shall now proceed to describe, present all the beauties which the most enthusiastic admirer of the country could desire. Proceeding from our original starting-point, the Market-place, we take a westerly direction, and, on arriving at the termination of the harbour, cross the bridge by which the river is spanned, and reach the south Quay. Turning to the left, and passing by the premises of the gas company, we ascend the steep road conducting to Douglas Head. Advancing eastward, we pass Taubman-terrace, Fort William, Fort Anne Hotel, Ravenscliffe, and Harold Tower, which have been already noticed. On gaining the summit of the headland, on which stands a substantial circular beacon, we suddenly obtain an incomparably beautiful view. A wide expanse of ocean lies before us: it is a prospect more like enchantment than reality.

> "Joyously
> The bright crests of innumerable waves
> Glance at the sun at once, as when the hands
> Of a great multitude are upward flung
> In acclamation."

In clear weather the towering summits of the mountains of Cumberland and Wales are distinctly visible. From this elevated position the town of Douglas, the full glory of the bay, and the surrounding country—famed for its beauty—will be most advantageously seen. We have also a remarkably fine view of the principal mountains of the isle, including South Barrull, Slieau Whuaillin, Greeba, Garraghan, Snaefell, Beinn-y-Phot, and North Bar-

rull.   A path, winding round the headland, conducts
to that picturesque spot, Pigeon's Cove, which will
amply repay a visit.   Let those who love pure air and
the uncontaminated beauties of nature repair to
Douglas Head.   Tradition states that it was once
"ful filled of fairie"—that

> "Of old the merry elves were seen
>   Pacing with printless foot the dewy green!"

On it, according to Train, are the chairs in which, it
is said, the nuns of the monastery of St. Bridget
were occasionally punished in ancient times.   "Over
the Howe of Douglas," he remarks, "there is a steep
rock of considerable height immediately above the
sea; about half way up this rock was a hollow resembling an elbow-chair, and near the top another
cavity somewhat similar.   On the slightest accusa-
tion, the poor nun was brought to the foot of this
rock when the sea had ebbed, and was obliged to
climb to the first chair, where she had to remain
till the tide again flowed and ebbed twice.   Those
who had given a greater cause of suspicion were
obliged to ascend to the second chair, and to sit
there for the same space of time.   Any one who
endured this trial, and descended unhurt, was
cleared of all aspersion that had been thrown upon
her."   Retracing our steps, we come back to the
bridge which spans the Douglas river.   Nearly
opposite to it is a bye-path conducting to a flagstaff
on the western summit of Douglas Head.   We recommend those who desire to obtain a magnificent
view of the picturesque vale of Braddan, of the
beautiful rural scenery of the island, of—

> "The hills
> Rock-ribbed and ancient as the sun—the vales
> Stretching in pensive quietness between;
> The venerable woods—rivers that move
> In majesty, and the complaining brooks
> That make the meadows green"—

to make the ascent. A recent writer thus describes the prospect:—"What a stretch of country lies exposed to the eye! You would think that it was one broad deep valley between this and yonder group of mountains; but if you were to attempt to traverse it, you would find that you had many a ridge to surmount, many a deep hollow to wade through. But what a thoroughly English scene (out of England though it be) it is, with its rich cultivation, its trees and green fields; its hamlets, and farmsteads, and innumerable villas; though possessing a grandeur all its own, derived from the presence of yonder mighty masses, which stand, as if giant sentinels, to guard its peace, plenty, and beauty. If you look attentively you may trace the gleaming river here and there—here in long lines straight or curving; there in mere dots, but always where the relieving splendour seems most wanted. Just, for all the world, is that river like a silver thread that has been drawn with consummate art through a rich web of darker colours. But now raise your eye to the mountains which stand out boldly in the full broad light of the sun, their bare sides all exposed, so that you might discern every prominence and detect every crevice; while the rugged outline of their forms is everywhere visible and clear, except of one solitary one, the summit of which lies hidden in a cloud, as mighty and apparently as solid as itself, but in hue, and blending of light and shadow, and in majesty, as it slowly moves along, far more grand and glorious."

Returning once more to the bridge, we turn to the left and enter the *Castletown-road*. Pursuing this pleasant road, a considerable portion of which runs under a green arcade of trees, we pass the ruins of an ancient bridge, connected with which is a wonderful legend. See Chapter XIII. The Nunnery and the site of the old Roman Catholic Chapel are afterwards passed: about half a mile beyond the latter is the junction of the two roads conducting to Castletown. Entering that on the left, we pass Ellenbrook, and Oakhill, where a neat little church has been erected, chiefly through the liberality of R. Crossfield, Esq. The next noticeable object is Hampton Court (a mansion situate a short distance from the road on the west side), about a quarter of a mile beyond which is a path leading to that delightful spot, Port Soderick, or *the bay in the south*—that is, as regards the bays of Ramsey and Douglas. It derives its name from the Old Norse "sudr," south, and "vik," an inlet or bay. There is here a picturesque vale. A beautiful streamlet flowing through it—

> "Sends forth glad sounds, and tripping o'er its bed
> Of pebbly sands, or leaping down the rocks,
> Seems, with continuous laughter, to rejoice
> In its own being."

To this enchanting locality multitudes resort in the summer months. A walk up the glen as far as Croga bridge will amply repay the tourist. The upper portion of this lovely and sequestered vale is luxuriously wooded, and the banks of the rivulet are covered with all sorts of wild flowers. In the rocks on the south side of the bay is a large cave with a very narrow entrance. On the headland above it, a fragment of an ancient cross, on which is sculptured the figure of a man on horseback, was found some time ago. Tradition states that an islet was submerged by enchantment in the sea near Port Soderick, and that it makes its appearance septennially. On the estate of Ballashamrock, adjacent to this charming little bay, was found, a few years since, a *kist-vaen*, in which was a skeleton, probably that of some valiant Scandinavian viking. In the cliffs about half a mile south of Port Soderick is a very extensive cavern, the entrance to which is concealed by a remarkable insulated rock. Many persons make

an excursion to Port Soderick by water, and thus
have an opportunity of surveying the coast scenery,
which is exceedingly picturesque.

Returning to Douglas, we cross the bridge and
ascend the short street, communicating with *Peel-
road*. Pursuing this road we pass by the Hermitage
and several other elegant mansions, occupied by
individuals of influence, and obtain a charming view
of the vale of Braddan. On its south side is the
Nunnery estate, to which a path on the left conducts.
Opposite to the first milestone stands Ballabrooie
(*Anglice*, the place of river banks), where a spa was
discovered many years ago : because of the incon-
venience arising from the resort of company, it was
blocked up. In a short time we reach the Quarter-
bridge, where there is an inn. Under this bridge
flows the Glass *(gray* or *clear)* river. Two roads
branch off at this point; that on the left to Castletown, that on the right to Onchan and Ramsey. The
first opening on the right-hand side of the latter
road conducts to Buck's-road, which has been already
noticed.)

Kirby House, the seat of his Honour Deemster
Drinkwater, next attracts attention. It is beautifully
situated on an eminence to the left, and is distin-
guished by the luxuriant plantations that surround it.
It was formerly the property of Colonel Wilks
(Governor of St. Helena), to whose charge the
Emperor Napoleon Bonaparte was committed in
1815. The road now crosses the meadow called
Port-e-Chee, which signifies in the Manx language
"The Haven of Peace." It is said that before the
Isle of Man was raised, by igneous agency, to its
present elevation, the sea flowed through the valley
between Douglas and Peel, and that this extensive
meadow was an inland loch or estuary. The mansion
on the right-hand side of it was one of the first
residences of the late Duke of Athole, prior to the

erection of Castle Mona. Advancing westward, we cross the bridge which spans the Doo, or *black* river, and arrive at

KIRK BRADDAN, which, although unmarked by any architectural beauty, will amply repay a visit. This church, an unpretending structure dedicated to St. Brandon (now called Braddan), is picturesquely situated on a rising ground, and is embosomed in a group of aged trees. It is twenty-seven yards long and seven broad, and has a low roof and narrow arched windows. At its west end is a square tower on which are two small bells in open arches: on the east side of this tower may be seen the date 1774. The church stands upon the site of the original edifice, the date of which is uncertain. It is recorded that in 1291 Bishop Marcus held a synod here, and that thirty-five new canons were then enacted. The extensive churchyard is densely crowded with graves. Amid the tombs near the west end of the church stands a lofty obelisk, the most conspicuous of the monuments in this interesting burial-place. It was erected to the memory of Lord Henry Murray, fifth son of John, Duke of Athole, and Lieutenant-Colonel Commandant of the regiment of Royal Manx Fencible Infantry. The inscription, on a piece of white marble inserted in it near the base, is as follows :—" This sincere testimonial of affection and deep regret for their commander and their friend is erected by the officers of the regiment.

> His saltem accumulem donis, et fungar inani
> Munere.—VIRGIL, *Æneid*, VI."

Close to the obelisk is the grave of Wordsworth's brother-in-law, Henry Hutchinson. The following epitaph, composed by the celebrated poet, is engraved upon the tombstone : " In memory of Henry Hutchinson, born at Penrith, Cumberland, 14th June, 1769. At an early age he entered upon a seafaring life, in the course of which, being of a thoughtful mind, he attained great skill and knowledge of his profession, and endured in all climates severe hardships with exemplary courage and fortitude. The latter part of his life was passed with a beloved sister upon this Island. He died at Douglas, the 23rd of May, 1839, much lamented by his kindred and friends, who have erected this stone to testify their sense of his mild virtues and humble piety." Among the other denizens of this silent city of the dead may be named the Rev. R. Brown, father of the Rev. Hugh Stowell Brown, of Liverpool; Captain Gill and Captain Quayle, of the Isle of Man Steam Packet Company; Dr. Oswald, F.A.S.; and Samuel Ally, an African who was born a slave, and indebted for freedom to the late Colonel Wilks (governor of St. Helena, and author of the "History of Mysore"), by whom the following epitaph was written:— "Samuel Ally, an African and native of St. Helena, died the 28th of May, 1822, aged 18 years. Born a slave, and exposed in early life to the corrupt influence of that unhappy state, he became a model of truth and probity for the more fortunate of any country or condition. This stone is erected by a grateful master to the memory of a faithful servant, who repaid the boon of liberty with unbounded attachment." The next noticeable object is an old tombstone which stands close to the principal entrance of the church. It bears this inscription, in characters particularly fresh and clear:—" Here underlyeth the body of the Reverend Mr. Patrick Thompson, minister of God's word forty years, at present Vicar of Kirk Bradan, aged sixty-seven anno 1673. Deceased yᵉ 24th April, anno 1689." This stone appears to have been erected sixteen years before the death of the eccentric vicar, who left a legacy of three pounds to the parish, forty shillings of which were directed " to be put in bank, and the interest to be forthcoming and truly payable to the poor from time to time during time!''

The chief objects of interest in this churchyard are the ancient sculptured monumental crosses with Scandinavian inscriptions. It is to be regretted that in bygone years no local concern was felt for the preservation of these precious relics of the past. In 1860 the writer of these pages persuaded the worthy vicar and the wardens of Kirk Braddan to erect a substantial mound in the centre of the churchyard and to place thereon three crosses, one of which has been irreparably injured. Of these the most remarkable

stands on the east end of the mound. It is fifty-seven inches high, eight inches broad at the base, and when complete, had a breadth of twelve inches at the top. Three sides of the shaft are decorated with serpents ingeniously interwoven. The fourth bears the following Runic inscription :—

"THURLABR NEAKI RISTI KRUS THANA AFT FIAK SUN SIN BRUTHUR SUN EABRS,"

i.e., "Thorlaf Neaki erected this cross to Fiach his son, the nephew (brother's son) of Jabr." The correct interpretation of this inscription was first given by Professor Munch. Of this cross Dr. Wilson remarks :— "The most thoroughly Scandinavian in character of all the Manx Runic crosses is the beautiful one which stands in the churchyard at Kirk Braddan. . .In nearly all the principal details, especially on the shaft, it differs entirely from the other Manx crosses, and corresponds to those on Scandinavian relics of the Iron Period. . .The shaft is decorated with the common dragon ornaments intrieately intertwined over its whole surface; thus greatly differing in style from the crosses wrought by the skilful hands of Gaut. . .The perforated head with interlaced ornamentation such as that which is here associated with the old dragon pattern and other Pagan devices of Scandinavia, is more directly traceable to the early Christian arts of Celtic Ireland." The proper name Fiach occurs often in ancient manuscripts relating to Irish history. See inscription No. 1, Chapter VI.

A fragment of another cross, beautifully ornamented with serpents intertwined, stands close to that which has been described. It is very similar to Fiach's cross, and is by no means of contemptible workmanship. This relic was long imbedded in mortar and stones above the lintel of a doorway in the steeple of the church, and was removed to the churchyard through the exertions of George Borrow, Esq., author of "The Bible in Spain." The inscription on it runs thus:—

"UTR RISTI KRUS THANA AFT FRAKA FATHUR SIN IN THUR-BIAURN SU[NR]...."

i.e., "Ottar erected this cross to his father Frakka, but Thorbjörn the son. . ." It may not be superfluous to remark that in Runic inscriptions "aft" (eft, eftir) literally signifies *after;* metaphorically *in memory of.* Professor Munch agrees with the present writer in reading the second name "Frakka:" that name frequently occurs in the sagas. A representation of this cross may be seen in the *Illustrated London News* of December 8, 1855.

Another ancient monumental cross stands upon the west end of the mound. It was formerly used as a step at the door of the church. Only one face is carved. This stone is about forty-two inches high and fourteen inches broad. The inscription is as follows:—

"THUR.....RAISTI KRUS THANN EFT UFAAG SUN KLINAIS,"

i.e., "Thor.....erected this cross to Ofeig Klinai-

D

sön." The last five runes in the first name have been almost obliterated, and are illegible. "Thor" enters into the composition of a large number of Scandinavian proper names, as Thorbjörn, Thorfinnr, Thorketil, Thorstein, Thorvaldr, &c. The translation of this inscription was first given by the present writer.

A fragment of a cross bearing the following inscription was found at Kirk Braddan :—

"ER ASKETIL VILTI I TRIGU AITHSAARA SIIN,"

thus rendered by Worsaae :—"Whom Asketil deceived in security, contrary to his pledge of peace."*
It is now in the Museum at Dissington, near Whitehaven. See inscription No. 3, Chapter VI.

At the base of the steeple stands a large cross

(represented in the annexed engraving), ornamented with knot-work and various grotesque animals. It is thirty-eight inches broad : the inscription has been obliterated. An old cross may be seen in the west wall of the tower, a few yards above the ground. Another stands near the west gate of the churchyard : it is decorated with knot-work,

---

* "I will here subjoin a very few *loca legis*, shewing what causes were decided by the Swedish Juries. I shall take an example from the Edzöris Balk of Landslagh. This section of the code treats of offences against the king's peace, in Swedish called Edzöre or Edsöre, a term which literally means OATH-SWEARING, *i.e.*, that oath by which the king obliges himself at his coronation to maintain peace in his dominions. The term Edzöre is somewhat vague, and of a very comprehensive signification in the Swedish codes, for it both means the king's peace itself, *i.e.*, that peace he has sworn to maintain ; and also the vast variety of offences committed against it ; for there are many offences, in other laws, not at all considered to be of the class of *crimina læsæ*, which in Swedish laws are brought under the class of Edzöri."—Repp on Ancient Juries, p. 96.

and perforated with four holes. A fragment of
another, twenty-four inches high and fourteen inches
broad, may be seen close to the last-mentioned cross.

Before proceeding further, we must ask the reader
to accompany us to the new cemetery, which is
adjacent to Kirk Braddan in the *Strang-road:* its
area is four acres, three of which are appropriated to
the public, and the other to those who desire private
ground as a last resting-place for their families.
Near its centre is the chapel wherein the funeral
service is read. In this cemetery repose the remains
of Martin, the distinguished painter. A friend of
the celebrated artist, G. H. Wood, Esq., remarks :—
" His annual visits to our isle, and ardent admiration
of its wild and picturesque scenery, may well be a
subject of honest pride to Manxmen ; but that in the
designs of Providence, this lonely and distant spot
should have been chosen for the final resting-place of
his honoured remains, is a melancholy privilege which
the natives of Mona could never have anticipated ;
and hallowed, no doubt, in their estimation will ever
be the place of his sepulture, where he will repose
by the side of some of his departed relatives, in the
cemetery on the hill, near the romantic churchyard of
Kirk Braddan, one of the spots he admired so much
and loved to visit; and henceforth the deathless name
of Martin, associated with that of our lonely isle,
like the great Napoleon's, linked with St. Helena,
will invest it with an interest and celebrity which will
endure to the end of time; and we may truly predict
that strangers from all parts of Europe, landing on
these shores, will, like pilgrims journeying to some
far-famed distant shrine, visit the grave of Martin,
and pay the sacred tribute of a tear to the memory
of immortal genius and sterling virtue."

Returning to the parish church, and crossing the
stile at the west side of the churchyard, we find our-
selves in the road which extends from Peel-road to

Mill Mount. In the orchard lying opposite to the stile some traces of an encampment—evidently of great antiquity—are discernible. Pursuing the road to the left, a few paces bring us to the mansion of Kirby. It is indebted for its name to an ancient village named Kirkeby (from the Danish *kirke*, church, and *by*, village) which was situated in the immediate vicinity of the parish church. Kirkeby is mentioned in a confirmation of the church lands made by Thomas, Earl of Derby, to the bishop of the isle, on the 28th of March, 1505. The first road branching to the right conducts to the vicarage of Braddan, and to the stone-circle (on Mount Murray) which some have erroneously supposed to be a Druidical temple.

The road extending from Kirby to Mill Mount is designated the *Saddle-road*. It derives its name from a curious stone called the fairy's saddle, which may be seen on the right-hand side. An old writer named Waldron says :—" Not far from Ballafletcher [Kirby] is the fairy's saddle, a stone so called, I suppose, from the similitude it has to a saddle. It seems to be loose on the edge of a small rock [it is now partly imbedded in a wall], and the wise natives of Man tell you it is every night made use of by the fairies, but on what kind of horses I could never find any who would inform me." Advancing along this pleasant rural road, we pass Ballaughton, and shortly afterwards arrive at Mill Mount, where there are several delightfully situated villas. In the garden of one of these a curious old coin was discovered a few years ago. On the obverse is represented a bishop with a crosier and crucifix; on the reverse a kneeling figure playing a harp, over which is a crown. The legend has been obliterated.

Crossing the high road and passing through a gateway, we enter a path which conducts to Pulrose Mill. After passing this, we cross a stile, pursue the footpath leading over a meadow, and arrive at the Nunnery grounds—one of the favourite resorts of the inhabitants of Douglas. Pedestrians in search of the picturesque should repair to this enchanting spot, where,

" Beneath th' umbrageous multitude of leaves,"

they may enjoy a delightful walk by the side of the crystal river that meanders through the richly-wooded Vale of Braddan. Its banks are shaded by fine trees, many of which almost dip their pendent branches in the clear stream. The Nunnery is famous for the historical reminiscences with which its name is associated. According to tradition it was founded in the sixth century by St. Bridget. The only vestige of the ancient edifice that now remains is part of the chapel, with its gothic windows and arched gateway, over which hangs a modern bell. The principal gate, we are informed, was only opened at the initiation of a nun, or at the death of the lady abbess. The following description, written many years since, will interest the reader:—" Few monasteries ever exceeded it either in largeness or fine building. There are still some of the cloisters remaining, the ceilings of which discover they were the workmanship of the most masterly hands; nothing in the whole creation but what is imitated in curious carvings on it.* The pillars supporting the arches are so thick as if that edifice was erected with a design to baffle the efforts of time, nor could it in more years than have elapsed since the coming of Christ have been so greatly defaced, had it received no injury but from time; but in some of the dreadful revolutions this island has sustained, it doubtless has

* " Two human figures, carved in oak, were discovered many years ago at the Nunnery. They may be seen at the *Herald* office.

suffered much from the outrage of the soldiers, as
may be gathered by the niches yet standing in the
chapel, which has been one of the finest in the world,
and the images of saints reposited in them being
torn out. Some pieces of broken columns are still
to be seen, but the greatest part have been removed.
The confessional chair also lies in ruins. There were
likewise a number of caverns under ground used as
places of penance." The prioress of this nunnery
was anciently a baroness of the isle, held courts in
her own name, and possessed great temporal, as well
as spiritual, authority. According to the "Chronicon
Manniæ," Robert Bruce, King of Scotland, spent a
night here in the year 1313.* A modern castellated
building—the seat of J. S. Goldie Taubman, Esq.,—
stands embosomed in the trees near the site of the
ancient priory: the extensive pleasure-grounds are as
charming as wealth can make them. After passing
the entrance of the mansion, we soon reach an
obelisk, standing on the right, a short distance from
the footpath. It was erected by public subscription
to the memory of Brigadier-General Thomas Leigh
Goldie (an uncle of the present proprietor of the
Nunnery estate), who fell at Inkermann on the 5th
of November, 1854. The gun at the base of the
monument was presented by the British Government:
it was captured from the Russians during the Cri-
mean war. Pursuing the footpath, we enter a handsome avenue of trees, of the richest foliage, after
passing through which we emerge from the Nunnery
grounds into Castletown-road, which has already
been noticed.

Once more we return to Braddan Church, and,

---

* "Robert, King of Scotland, anchored at Ramsö, with a
numerous fleet, on the 18th day of May ; and, on the Sunday
following, went to the monastery of Dubh-glass, where he spent
the night."

taking a westerly direction, proceed along Peel-road. About a mile from the church stand the Union Mills (the proprietor of which is Mr. W. Dalrymple), where woollen cloths of excellent quality are made. In the thriving village of the Union Mills stands the Dalrymple Memorial Chapel, a handsome little edifice, erected by public subscription in 1863 as a tribute of respect and affection to the memory of the late Mr. James Dalrymple, the philanthropic father of the above-mentioned gentleman. Pursuing the path branching to the left, we come, after a pleasant walk of about a mile and a quarter, to a wide macadamized road : turning to the right and entering this road, a very beautiful and extensive rural prospect is obtained :

> " The mountains that infold,
> In their wide sweep, the coloured landscape round,
> Seem groups of giant kings, in purple and gold,
> That guard the enchanted ground."

After proceeding a mile and a quarter further, we arrive at the northern extremity of the hill of Mount Murray, where may be seen the largest stone circle in the island. It will be noticed in our description of the parish of Marown. Turning to the right, we enter the road which conducts through a charming and fertile valley designated Glen Darragh. Advancing northward, in Marown, we reach the Peel-road, and proceed again to our starting-point, Kirk Braddan.

The northern portion of the parish of Braddan demands some notice. Entering the Strang-road, we pass the new cemetery and the handsome parochial school. The first opening on the right conducts to Tromode (in Onchan), which will well repay a visit. The Glass (gray or clear) river is here spanned by a substantial ivy-covered bridge. The chief objects of interest in this place are the remains of an ancient

fortification called Castleward, the little chapel-of-
ease, and the palatial residence of W. F. Moore,
Esq. The manufacture of sail-cloth and linen is
prosecuted with remarkable vigour in this picturesque
locality by the above-mentioned gentleman.

Returning to the Strang-road, and proceeding
westward, we pass the entrance of Leece Lodge, and
arrive at the village to which this road is indebted
for its name. At this point two roads branch off;
that on the left conducts to the Union Mills, that on
the right leads to East Baldwin and the Abbey Lands.
About half-a-mile beyond the village, on the estate
named Camlork, may be seen the ruins of an ancient
Treen chapel, situate in a field on the right-hand side
of the road. We next come to Mount Rule, and
turning to the right, enter the road conducting to
West Baldwin (where there is a lead mine) and to
that delightful locality, Injebreck. Let those who
are

> "Enamoured of sequestered scenes,
> And charmed with rural beauty,"

repair to this picturesque and secluded spot. An excellent mountain road conducts from Injebreck to the
village of Michael: another leads to Beinn-y-Phot
and Snaefell. In returning, we recommend the
tourist to ascend the steep road on the left, leading
to the chapel-of-ease, dedicated to St. Luke, which
stands upon the site of an old Treen chapel called
Keil Abbane. An ancient Tynwald mound may be
seen in this locality (see Rev. Mr. Airey's edition of
Feltham, and the Statute Book, p. 6). On gaining
the summit of the hill, the visitor should turn to the
right, proceed southward a short distance, enter the
first opening on the left, and descend into East Baldwin. Here he will find a good road, extending
northward to the mountains and southward to the
Strang. A pretty rivulet flows through the valley,

and the surrounding scenery is at once beautiful and romantic. The inhabitants of Baldwin relate some very wonderful stories concerning those remarkable Liliputian beings, the Manx fairies. Pursuing the road on the right we pass the Baldwin paper-mills, cross a bridge, and in a short time arrive at the Strang, whence, proceeding to the left, we return to our starting-place, the parish church.

We now proceed to describe the parish of—

CONCHAN, or Onchan, which is bounded on the north by Lonan, on the south and east by the sea, and on the west by Braddan. It derives its name from Conchan, or Conanus (a bishop of the island in the seventh century), to whom the parish church is dedicated. This parish, from its vicinity to Douglas, is very pleasant, affording from its higher ground charming sea-views. The prominent object in the village is the church, at the west end of which stands a tower, surmounted by a spire. The style of architecture is early English. Scattered about the churchyard are several Runic crosses. Of these the most remarkable may be seen near the centre of the area on the north side of the church; it is very elaborately sculptured. Grotesque animals are carved on each side of the shaft of the cross. The inscription has been obliterated. A large cross, on which is sculptured knotwork, lies on the ground near the north side of the churchyard. A fragment of a small cross, beautifully carved, stands close to the north wall. On another cross, which was formerly in this churchyard, was the following inscription :—

" . . . ITRA ES LAIFA FUSTRA GUTHAN SON ILAN."

Professor Munch says : " The last four words are evidently, transposed into normal othography: '*fostra gothan, sun illan*,' i.e., '*educatorem bonum, filium malum;*' curious words, showing that these inscriptions were not only panegyrics. Whether, however, both

epitheta refer to one person or to two, is impossible
to say, as we do not have the whole. *Leifa,* accus.
form of ' *Leifi,*' seems to be the name of the person
or one of the persons in question. Of ' itra es '
nothing satisfactory can be made out."

I cannot profess myself satisfied with this interpretation. It appears to me that the second and third
words form the proper name Isleif (Asleif, Esleif);
and that the last three ought to be translated "God-
win the son of Ilan " (Alan ?). See inscription No.
15, Chapter VI.

In the garden of St. Catherine's, adjacent to the
church, are two Runic crosses. One of these bears
the following inscription, which is imperfect, a
portion of the stone having been broken off:—

> " KRUS . . . . SUNR RAISTI EFT KUINU SINA MYRGIALU M . . . .
> UGIGAD AUKR ATHIGRID . . . . THURITH RAIST RUNER . . . .
> ISU KRIST,"

i.e., " (A. B.) son of (C. D.) erected (this) cross to
Mirgiol his wife, mother of Hugigud, Haukr, (and)
Athigrid . . . . Thurid engraved (these) runes . . . .
Jesus Christ." The word *modur* (mother) probably
followed the name Mirgiol. The word *thesser* un-
doubtedly followed *runer.* See inscription No. 17,
Chapter VI.

The Rev. Mr. Cumming says:—" At the head of
the stone, on one face we have, very distinct, running
upwards, the word ' CRU ' for *crus,* cross; just below,
in the upper limb of the inscribed cross, written
downwards, the Runes ' ISUCRIST,' Jesus Christ; on
the left side, at the foot of the cross, the word
' THURITH,' the maker's name; considerably below
which, towards the edge, the words ' RAIST RUNER,'
engraved the Runes. On the other face of the slab,
on the left-hand side of the shaft near the edge,
running upwards, is ' SUNR : RAISTI : AFTIR : SUN :
SINA :' *i.e.,* ' (N. N.'s) son erected this to his son ;'

and then, running downwards, the name 'MURKIBLU.'
On the right-hand side of the shaft, running upwards, are apparently the words ' UGIGAT : ASUIR :
ATHIGRIT :' and then running down again, very
faintly, the letters 'AM : I.' It is to be noted that
the Manx Runes for U and R are very much alike,
that a small stroke will change A into B or E, and that
the Runes for G and C, D and F, are the same. Hence
Mr. W. Kneale has read ' Murkiblu' *Myrgialu*,
'Athigrit' *Athigrid*, 'Ugigat' *Hugigud*, 'Asuir'
Haukr, and ' *Sun* ' Kuinu; translating the inscription, '(A. B.) son of (C. D.) erected (this) cross
to Mirgiol, his wife, mother of Hugigud, Haukr,
(and) Athigrid . . . . Thurid engraved (these) Runes
. . . . Jesus Christ.' "*

The other cross, or rather fragment of a cross, is

---

* Upon the comparative merits of these two versions we
leave the reader to decide for himself. The translation of Professor Munch (who received copies of the Manx Runic inscriptions from the Rev. Mr. Cumming and J. J. A. Worsaae), is as
follows :—

"Cross at Kirk Onchan—(*a*) on the top: . . CRVS . ., *i.e.*,
kross—*crucem*. (*b*) Lower down . . : . . ISVCRIST, *i.e.*, Jesu
Krist. (*c*) Below on the right arm: THVRITH RAIST RVNAR;
Thuridr reist runar, *i.e.*, *Thurida sculpsit literas*. On the other
side, (*d*) below on the right arm: . . . SVNR RAISTI AFTIR SVN
SINA MVROIBLV; here it seems likely that the B in MVRCIBLV is
turned by a mistake to the wrong side, and ought to have been
an a; MVRCIALV would be Myrgjalu, Myrgjölu, accus. of a not
uncommon feminine Gaelic name, written in ancient records
sometimes *Muriella*. SINA (lat. *suam*), however, and the feminine name Muriella cannot agree with SVN; I might therefore
be inclined to think, that SVN is totally misspelled by a careless
or ignorant engraver, and ought to be CVNV; the whole would
then run thus: . . . . sunr reisti (kross) eftir konu sina
Myrgjölu— . . . *filius erexit (crucem) post uxorem suam Muriel-
lam*. (*e*) Below on the left arm: VCICAT ASVIR ATHICRIT AM
NTH. This seems to us wholly unintelligible, and is, perhaps,
Gaelic."—See Professor Munch's edition of the *Chronicon Manniæ*, p. xxiv. The first edition of this guide-book was printed
before that valuable work reached England.

ornamented with graceful sculptures : on the right-hand side of the shaft is carved the figure of an animal with extended jaws.

The Onchan Nursery Grounds, which are beauti-fully laid out, will amply repay a visit. Glen Crutchery (the Harper's Glen) is not far from the village. Adjacent to it is the mansion of Bema-hague, the residence of his Excellency the Lieu-tenant-Governor. A road conducts from the church to the pretty creek of Growdale; another leads to Onchan Harbour, whence we can proceed, by a path along the cliffs, to Derby Castle at the the north of Douglas Bay.

We now advance northward beyond the village. The first road on the left-hand side conducts to Glen Doo, Cronk-ny-Mona, and Tromode. In a short time we enter the parish of—

LONAN, which is bounded on the north by Maug-hold, on the south by Onchan, on the east by the sea, and on the west by Onchan and Lezayre. In 1609, according to an old manuscript in the possession of the Earl of Derby, there was "Noe tenant within that parish because of the barren soyle there." Near to the fifth milestone, a road branching to the right conducts to the picturesque little haven of Growdale, not far from which stands the old parish church. It is dedicated to St. Lonan or Lomanus, who was bishop of the island in the sixth century. On a mound of earth, adjacent to it, may be seen a fragment of a small cross. In the churchyard is a very large monumental cross with its end wedged into a groove of a ponderous flat stone. A fragment of another beautiful cross is built into the wall at the gate of the churchyard.

Retracing our steps to the main road, we advance northward. In a field on the east side of the road, not far from the sixth milestone, is the remarkable sepulchral monument called "The Cloven Stones."

It consists of two stones about six feet high, one of which has been cleft in twain from top to bottom.

These stones formed part of an ancient Scandinavian monument, which was thus described by Wood in 1811:—"Nearly two miles on the Douglas side of Laxey near the road, are about twelve stones placed in a form somewhat oval. Just beyond the oval, and at one end of it, facing N.N.E., are two stones six feet high, one of which is cloven from top to bottom: the other stones are from two to three feet high. The mount on which they all stand is three or four feet high. The centre of the mount has an excavation, seven feet long, three feet wide for about one-third of the length, and two feet for the remainder. The stones are of hard clay-slate." Near this singular tomb is an old fortified hill. A path on the right conducts to the picturesque creek called Garwick, into which flows the Gliongawne rivulet. The new church of Lonan, a neat structure in the early English style of architecture, stands on a hill to the left: at its west end is a lofty pinnacled tower.

Continuing our journey, we arrive at—

LAXEY, which is situate in a lovely and romantic
glen, and girt about by an amphitheatre of undu-
lating verdant hills.   Fair to look on is this
village, thus nestled in a broad and fertile valley,
beautifully wooded and watered, and overshadowed
by the towering Snaefell, the loftiest mountain in the
isle.   Laxey was unquestionably a Scandinavian
settlement.   It derives its name from the rivulet (Old
Norse, "Laxá," *i.e.*, salmon river), which flows
through this picturesque glen.   According to Speed,
it was a place of considerable importance in the
sixteenth century.   It is celebrated for its mines of
lead, copper, and silver, which are very productive.
About one hundred and twenty tons of lead (each ton
containing from fifty to sixty ounces of silver), thirty
tons of copper, and from three to four hundred tons
of blende are obtained per month.   The depth of the
mines is about two hundred and fifteen fathoms.
The plant includes all the most improved mining
machinery of the most powerful description.   The
great water wheel (of 200 horse power), supposed to
be the largest in the world, was constructed by Mr.
Casement, a native of the island, for the purpose of
pumping the water out of the mines.   It forms a very
conspicuous object in the lovely glen where it is
situate.   Two revolutions per minute keep the mines
clear of water.   It will pump 250 gallons per minute,
if required, from a depth of 400 yards.   The circumference of the wheel is 217 feet 6 inches, the diameter
72 feet six inches, the breadth 6 feet; the length of
shaft 17 feet, the diameter 21 inches, weight 10 tons ;
the length of crank 5 feet, of stroke 10 feet, stroke
of the beam at the mine pump 8 feet.   The wheel
is supported in its bearings by a substantial and
elegant structure of masonry and iron, arranged in
open arches and galleries.   The upper gallery (the
end of which, in front of the masonry, is decorated
with the "three legs," the well-known armorial

bearings of the Isle of Man) is on a level with the shaft. Staircases winding round a white pillar conduct to the balcony, which commands a noble prospect of the glen. The water (which is conveyed underground, in pipes two feet in diameter, from the reservoirs situate on an adjacent hill), after rising up the centre of the massive pillar, is carried by a duct under the balcony over the wheel, and pouring on to it, returns in the opposite direction; for the wheel is what is termed a "breast-shot," and the water does not pass right over the top as an "over-shot." A viaduct about two hundred yards in length, carries the connecting-rods for working the pumps from the the wheel to the shaft of the mine. The inauguration of this huge water-wheel (which is called the "Lady Isabella," in honour of the lady of the Hon. Charles Hope) was celebrated by a grand *fête* on the 27th of September, 1854. A small and handsome chapel-of-ease, erected by the mining company, stands near the centre of the village.

The lover of romantic scenery ought not to leave this locality without visiting the far-famed Glen Roy, a charming spot, which is much resorted to by tourists.

Laxey Bay is two miles in width: on the south beach may be seen Lord Henry's well. About a mile to the north of the bay, under the rocks, is an unexplored cavern.

In ascending Laxey Hill, a stone circle on the right hand attracts attention. Not far from it, on the left-hand side, is a dilapidated Scandinavian cairn designated "King Orry's Grave!" The proprietor of the ground on which it stands, on removing some of the stones, discovered a vault fifteen feet square, containing a *kist-vaen* of most singular construction, inside of which were found the bones and teeth of a horse. Some years ago an ancient and very valuable gold bracelet was discovered in a garden situate in the vicinity of Laxey.

The Laxá, or salmon river, is mentioned in an old martial poem, of which we possess a copy. A few extracts relative to events which occurred in the eleventh century, will not be unacceptable to the reader:—"Tatwallin ended his song, the chiefs arose from the great plain; they assemble their troops on the banks of Lexy. Ceormond with the green spear, martialled his band: he deduced his lineage from Woden, and displayed the shield of Penda. Strong as the tower of Pendragon on the hill, furious as the souls of unburied warriors; his company were all chiefs. Upon the high hills he encountered Moryon; like dashing waves, they rushed to the war; their swords rained blood to the valley beneath. Moryon, wild as the winter's wind, raged in the fight: the pointed javelin quivered in his breast, he rolled down the high hill. Son of Woden, great was thy might, by thy hand the two sons of Osmor fell to the valley. How are thy warriors stretched upon the bank of the Lexy, like willows! . . . . . . Godred retires to the bank of the Lexy; the foe followed behind, but were driven back with shame. On the banks of the Lexy the warriors are scattered like broken oaks . . . . . . On the rushy moor of Rossin they astonish the foe, and join in the war. There fought Godred Crovan, death sat on his sword, the yelling breath of the dying foe shook his banner; his shield, the stream of Lexy, which surrounds the dark-brown wood, and shines at the noon of day; his anlace dropped blood and tore through the helmets of the foe like the red lightning of the storm."

While he is in Laxey, the visitor should ascend Snaefell (*i.e.*, Snow-mountain, from the Old Norse *snae*—with the masculine termination *snaer*—snow, and *fiall* or *fell*, mountain), which rises 2024 feet above the level of the sea. The prospect from its summit is scarcely equalled, for extent and beauty, by any in the United Kingdom. It is remarkable for including the several parts of the British dominions; the ranges of Snowdon and of Cumberland being visible to the southward and eastward, the mountains of Morne and Fairhead appearing on the west side, and the Mull of Galloway, with the elevation of Criffell, rising in the northern horizon. An excellent view of the island itself is also obtained.

Cowley, the poet, in his "Discourse by way of Vision, concerning the Government of Oliver Cromwell," after describing the funeral of the great Protector, says :—"I retired back to my chamber, weary, and I think more melancholy than any of the mourners. Where I began to reflect upon the whole life of this prodigious man, and sometimes I was filled with horror and detestation of his actions, and sometimes I inclined a little to reverence and admiration of his courage, conduct, and success; till by these different motions and agitations of mind, rocked as it were asleep, I fell at last into this Vision, or if you please to call it but a Dream, I shall not take it ill. . .But sure it was no dream; for I was suddainly transported afar off, (whether in the body or out of the body, like St. Paul, I know not), and found myself on the top of that famous hill in the Island Mona, which has the prospect of three great and not long since most happy kingdoms. As soon as ever I look'd on them, they not long since struck upon my memory, and called forth the sad representation of all the sins, and all the miseries that had overwhelmed them these twenty years. And I wept bitterly for two or three hours, and when my present stock of moisture was all wasted, I fell a sighing for an hour more, and as soon as I recovered from my passion the use of speech and reason, I broke forth, as I re-

member, (looking upon England) into this complaint
[here follow eight stanzas]. I think I should have
gone on, but that I was interrupted by a strange and
terrible apparition, for there appeared to me (arising
out of the earth, as I conceived), the figure of a man
taller than a Gyant, or indeed, than the shadow of
any Gyant in the evening. His body was naked, but
that nakedness adorn'd, or rather deform'd all over,
with several figures, after the manner of the ancient -
Britons, painted upon it. . .His eyes were like burning brass, and there were three crowns of the same
metal (as I guest) and that look'd as red-hot too upon
his head. . .Though this sudden, unusual, and dreadful object might have quelled a greater courage than
mine, yet so it pleased God, (for there is nothing
bolder than a man in a vision) that I was not at all
daunted, but ask'd him resolutely and briefly, What
art thou ? and he said, I am called, The North-west
Principality, His Highness the Protector of the
Common-wealth of England, Scotland, and Ireland,
and the dominions belonging thereunto, for I am
that Angel to whom the Almighty has committed the
government of these three kingdoms which thou seest
from this place, &c."

We must now ask the reader to accompany us from
Douglas to the parish of—

MAROWN. Entering Peel-road, we proceed westward, pass Braddan Church and the Union Mills,
and soon reach Marown, which is surrounded by
hills, and bounded by Braddan, Santon, Malew,
Patrick, and German. A little beyond the fourth
milestone is the new parish church, a handsome
edifice on the south side of the road. We then come
to Crosby, *i.e.*, the cross village. One of the principal objects of interest in the parish may be seen a
short distance beyond the fifth milestone. We allude
to an ancient church dedicated to St. Trinion, or
Ninian. It is situate in a field on the north side of

the road, and is reported to be a votive edifice, built
to fulfil a vow made by a person in imminent danger
of shipwreck; who or what he was, and when the
vow was made, or the church built, tradition does not
say: it, however, relates that the present ruinous
state of the building was owing to malice of a mischievous *buggane*, or evil spirit, who, for want of
better employment, amused himself with throwing
off the roof, which frolic he so often repeated, that at
length the edifice was abandoned.   The subjoined

sketch is a view of St. Trinion's in its present state.
An amusing legend connected with this ruinous
church will be found in Chapter XIII.   Adjacent to
the church is the Round Meadow (called by the
Manx *yn cheance rhunt*), concerning which a wonderful story is related.   See Chapter XIII.   Every
tourist with leisure at command should ascend Greeba,
whose southern summit is 1373 feet above the level
of the sea: from this elevated point, a beautiful and
extensive prospect is obtained.   Picnic parties, in the
summer, are frequently formed to visit this delightful
spot.   At the base of the mountain are Greeba

Tower and Greeba Castle, situated amidst beautiful plantations and pleasure-grounds.

Retracing our steps to the picturesque village of Crosby, we diverge to the right and pursue the road conducting to the ancient parish church, which in its time appears to have enjoyed great celebrity. According to an old traditionary ballad, here repose the remains of St. Lomanus, St. Conanus, and St. Rooney. Part of the porch was brought from St. Trinion's. A large antique font stands near it.

Proceeding southward from this ancient structure, we come to the old vicarage, not far from which, in a field near the Garth, is a rude stone chair: two of the slabs forming the back of this seat are marked with a deeply-incised cross. It has been called, though without the slightest authority, St. Patrick's Chair; and zealous archæologists believe that the patron saint of Ireland, to whom some have attributed the introduction of Christianity into the Isle of Man, sat in it to bless the people. There is no evidence that St. Patrick ever was in Man. This singular relic is, perhaps, an ancient Keltic inauguration-chair: here, on the accession of an *oir-righ* or sub-king, the installatory ceremony may have been performed.

Returning to Peel-road, and proceeding eastward, we again pass through the village of Crosby. We now purpose to visit Glen Darragh, which has been noticed in our account of Braddan. To reach the beautiful "Vale of Oaks," we must deviate from the Peel-road, and pursue the road which branches to the right near the fourth milestone. Treen chapels stand on the neighbouring estates of Ballachrink, Ballalough, Ballingan, and Ballaquinney - mooar. After advancing southward nearly two miles, we arrive at the northern extremity of the hill of Mount Murray, where may be seen a very remarkable monument of antiquity. It is situate in a field on the left-hand side, not far from the road, and con-

sists of stones placed upright at regular distances, forming a circle of about forty feet in diameter. To the east of it were formerly two mounds (fifteen feet from each other), constructed of earth and stones, and forming a semi-circle. Some imaginative antiquaries suppose this circular work to have been a temple of the Druids, an idea for which there is no foundation. The stone circle is represented in the foregoing woodcut. It is probably a Scandinavian place of sepulture of the latest period of heathenism, or what is termed the Iron Age. Opposite to the stone circle, on the right-hand side, is "Slieau Chiarn," or the "Mountain of the Lord." The neighbouring scenery is peculiarly fine.

Proceeding still southward, we reach a point where several roads meet (that on the left conducting to the Union Mills and Kirk Braddon; that on the right to Foxdale), and approach the estate called Balla Nicholas, on which are the remains of two ancient circular forts. On the mountains of Archallaghan, in this parish, the antiquary will find several barrows.

The next turning on the left conducts to the parish of St. Anne, or Santon, which is bounded by Malew,

Braddan and the sea.   On the right we pass an
estate called Ferk, where there is a very remarkable
old fort, commanding an extensive view.   Mount
Murray mansion, seated amidst thriving plantations,
is adjacent.   Turning to the right and pursuing the
new Castletown-road, we arrive at Ballalona-bridge,
which is said to be the scene of his satanic majesty's
frequent exploits, on which account the natives seldom
venture over it after dark.   The neighbouring valley,
through which flows the Santonburn, has many
attractions for the tourist, and will amply repay a
visit.   The parish church, an unpretending little
building, dedicated to St. Anne, is situated about
half a mile from the shore.   A church stood upon
the site of the present structure in the thirteenth
century.   Feltham says, "An old stone with some
characters similar to Roman capitals thereon was dug
up in the churchyard at a very great depth."   This
stone has unfortunately disappeared : a representation
of it was given by the late Dr. Oswald in a communication to the Scottish Society of Antiquaries.
Speaking of this inscription, the late Dr. Jamieson
says : "I read it as barbarous Latin for AVITUM
MONOMENTUM, signifying the monument or tomb
belonging to ancestors.   The characters seem pretty
nearly to resemble the old Teutonic as given by
Astle, Tab. 1, p. 64."
    Leaving the church and entering the old Castletown-
road, we advance eastward.   The first opening on
the right-hand conducts to the picturesque creek
designated Greenwick, close to which are two old
fortifications.   "In the records of the Duchy of
Lancaster," says Train, "the adjoining lands are
called Thorkilstadt, supposed to be derived from the
celebrated sea-king, Thorkel."   A fine specimen
of the sepulchral barrow, called Cronk-ny-Marroo,
i.e., Hill of the Dead, stands on the sea-cliff; it is an
oblong mound, forty feet long, twenty feet broad,

and twelve feet high. Not far from Greenwick is another inlet designated Saltwick: the rocks here are grand.

Retracing our steps to the high-road, and advancing in a northerly direction we pass a small stone circle, situate in a field on the left-hand side; it is on the estate of Ballakelly. After proceeding about a mile further, we enter the parish of Braddon, which has already been described.

CHAPTER VIII.

DESCRIPTION OF CASTLETOWN, AND THE PARISHES OF MALEW, ARBORY, AND RUSHEN.

"I pray you, let us satisfy our eyes
With the memorials, and the things of fame,
That do renown this city.
                              SHAKESPEARE.

CASTLETOWN, or Balla-Chashtal (anciently called Russin), the metropolis of the Isle of Man, the military head-quarters, and the seat of government, is situated on the western side of an extensive bay, of horse-shoe form, in a fertile and beautiful district, the climate of which is much lauded. The town is intersected by the Silverburn. The market-place, a fine area of considerable extent, is adorned with a Doric column fifty feet high, erected in 1836, to the memory of the late Lieutenant-Governor Cornelius Smelt: here may be seen the Castle, the Custom-House, the Barracks, the George Hotel, the Union Hotel, the Post-Office, and St. Mary's Church.

The principal attraction of this notable old town (which is in the parish of Malew), is the venerable fortress, once deemed impregnable, to which it is indebted for its name. Some attribute the building of this ancient structure to Gudröd, the son of "King Orry." We are of opinion that it only dates from the twelfth century. Many writers have asserted that

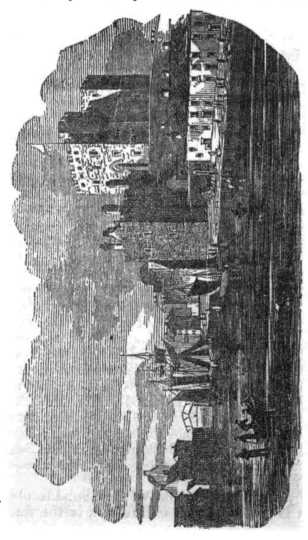

Rushen Castle bears a very striking resemblance to that of Elsinore; but Samuel Harris, Esq. (the worthy High Bailiff of Douglas), who has travelled in Denmark, assures us that this statement is quite erroneous. The late Professor Forbes declared that the Castle of Elsinore is "no more like Castle Rushen in Man (to which it had been compared) than a dog is like a donkey." This building is of a quadrangular form, with towers of the same shape on its four sides. The height of the north or flag tower is eighty feet. The south tower contains the clock, which was presented in 1597 by Queen Elizabeth. The walls of the keep are from seven to twelve feet thick. The ramparts are twenty-five feet high and nine feet thick, battlemented round by a covered way on the top, and defended by seven square machicolated towers, a ditch or fosse (which has been filled up many years), and a glacis of an irregular form, supposed to have been built by Cardinal Wolsey, when that celebrated ecclesiastic was guardian to Edward, third Earl of Derby. As the visitor rambles about this remarkable fortress, he has pointed out to him the Rolls' Office, the Court House and Council Chamber, the ancient kitchen, known by its large fireplace, the banqueting-hall, and various other apartments which were required when the kings of Man resided here. In 1265, according to the "Chronicon Manniæ," Magnus Olafsön, the last of the descendants of Gudröd Crovan, and the last Norwegian king who filled the throne, died here. In 1313 Robert Bruce, King of Scotland, laid siege to this castle, which was defended by Lord Dungawi Macdougal: notwithstanding the immense force of the beleaguering army, six months passed away before it capitulated. No person could be admitted as a soldier into the castle until he had provided himself with a bow and arrows, with a sufficient doublet or habergeon, a sword and buckler, spurs and a saddle. In after

times only a musket or *cavillier*, either with firelock
or matchlock, was required. In 1430 Henry Byron,
the Lieutenant-Governor of Man, caused six representatives to be sent from each of the sheadings, to
attend a Court between the gates of the castle; from
each of these six individuals he selected four, making
up the number of twenty-four, and by that means, if
not founding, at least re-establishing the House of
Keys. Castle Rushen was the occasional residence of
the Stanleys. James, the seventh Earl of Derby,
lived here from 1643 to 1651. His heroic wife, who
was resident with her family in the castle at the time
when Man was surrendered to the Republican army
under Birch and Duckenfield, was detained prisoner
here till the Restoration; but her captivity was
softened by the civility and generosity of the officers.
James, the tenth Earl of Derby, lived here during
the winter of 1712.

A spiral stone staircase in the inner keep conducts
to the flag tower, which, as we have already stated,
is eighty feet high. "The view in the clear twilight
from the top," says Dr. Neale, "is superb. Looking
south, far over the waters, you catch Penmæn Mawr,
like a cloud in the distance, but most clearly visible
without a telescope; to the right, the savage cliffs of
the Calf, and the more stupendous outline of Spanish
Head, raising themselves against the gold of the
setting sun: across them, Slieve Donard in Down,
and the high land around Dundrum Bay; to the
north, the whole chain of Manx mountains, from
purple North Barrule, by royal Snaefell, and Black
Boin-y-phot, and double-headed Garrahan, and
pyramid-like Greeba, and lonely Slieau Whuaillan,
down to South Barrule, gorgeous in the sunset, and
uttermost Cronk-ny-Irey-Lhàa. Then a little to the
east, darkness is closing in around Scawfell Pikes and
Ennerdale." A celebrated antiquary (Grose)
remarks: "As this fortress has at different times

sustained several sieges, the repairs of the damages
damages sustained must have somewhat altered its
interior parts, though in all probability the keep of
the castle itself is still in its original form."

The sittings of the Keys, who form the lower branch
of the Tynwald Court, are held in a small square
building, possessing no architectural pretensions,

situate near the gate of the
castle. In the garden of Lorn
House, adjacent to the draw-
bridge which spans the inner
harbour, is a Roman altar; it
was brought to the Isle of Man
more than one hundred years
ago, from the Roman station of
Ellenborough, near Maryport,
in Cumberland.

We now pursue the road
that conducts to Douglas. The
first turning on the right leads
to Derby Haven. Entering
this road, we soon reach that
noble educational institution,
KING WILLIAM'S COLLEGE, which is situated in a
beautiful and highly salubrious locality, at the head
of Castletown bay. It is well fitted up so as to ensure
the health and comfort of the students. The course
of education embraces the Greek and Latin classics,
Hebrew, modern languages, the mathematics, &c.,
and the doctrines and duties of Christianity, as taught
by the united Churches of England and Ireland.
Pupils are expressly prepared for entrance at Oxford,
Cambridge, and Trinity College, Dublin. Attached
to King William's College is a museum which possesses
a collection of all the known rocks, minerals, and
fossils of the Isle of Man.

At Hango Hill (a Scandinavian appellation)
adjacent to the college, may be seen the ruins of

Mount Strange, said to have been a fort built by
. James, the seventh Earl of Derby. Here William
Christian, called by the Manx Illiam Dhone, *i.e.*, the
fair-haired William, was judicially murdered in the
year 1662. In the parish register of Malew we read
that "Mr. William Christian, of Ronaldsway, late
Receiver, was shott to death at Hango Hill the 2nd
of January, 1662. He died most penitently and most
curragiously—made a good end—prayed earnestly—
and, next day, was buried in the chancel of Kirk
Malew." See Chap. II. Proceeding eastward from
Hango Hill, we come to the peninsula of Langness,
which derives its name from the Old Norse words
langr and *nœs*, signifying the long naze or promontory;
it forms the eastern side of Castletown Bay. The rocks
near the southern extremity of this peninsula are called
the Skerranes, in which name we meet with the Old
Norse *skér;* these rocks are only visible at low water.
On the eastern side of Langness may be seen several
caves and a very remarkable natural arch. At its
northern extremity is St. Michael's Islet, which is
connected by a causeway with Langness. On this
islet is an old ruinous church, used as a place of
interment for Roman Catholics; the date of the
edifice is unknown. Not far from it stands a circular
dilapidated fort, the walls of which are about eight
feet thick; over the entrance is a stone sculptured
with an earl's coronet, and the date 1645. Chaloner
asserts that this structure was erected by the seventh
Earl of Derby. St. Michael's Islet forms the eastern
shore of

DERBY HAVEN, the best natural harbour in the
island. The village of Derby Haven is contiguous to
Ronaldsway (Rögnvaldsvagr), the scene of many
sanguinary battles in the thirteenth and fourteenth
centuries. Not far from this locality is the beautiful
inlet designated Cas-na-awin, *i.e.*, the Bay of the River;
here the Santonburn disembogues itself into the sea.

Retracing our steps to the high road conducting to Douglas, we proceed northward, pass the Creggans— the well-cultivated farm belonging to J. C. Ewart, Esq., late Member of Parliament for Liverpool—and in a short time arrive at

BALLASALLA (which is about two miles from Castletown), the largest and most populous village in the island, and formerly a place of considerable importance.* Contiguous to this village stand the venerable ruins of the ABBEY OF RUSHEN or RUSSIN. This ancient abbey is romantically situated at the foot of a wood-crowned hill, on the banks of a crystal stream descending from South Barrull. It was founded in 1134 by Olaf, King of Man, and third son of Gudröd Crovan. According to the "Chronicon Manniæ," which was written here, that monarch gave to Ivo or Evan, abbot of Furness, a portion of his lands in Man towards building an abbey in a place called Russin; he bestowed on it one third of the tithes of the island for the education of youth and relief of the poor. He dedicated the abbey to the

---

* Three miles from this village northwards is the Chapel of Ease, dedicated to St. Mark; it was erected in 1772. Not far from it, on the banks of a placid stream, stood the old fortress which is described by Sir Walter Scott in "Peveril of the Peak." "In former times," says the celebrated novelist, "a Danish or Norwegian fastness had stood here, called the Black Fort, from the colour of a huge heathy hill, which, rising behind the building, appeared to be the boundary of the valley, and to afford the source of the brook." A large stone called Gudröd Crovan's stone, formerly stood near it. "The monumental stone, designed to commemorate some feat of an ancient king of Man, which had been long forgotten, was erected on the side of a narrow lonely valley, or rather glen, secluded from observation by the steepness of its banks, upon a projection of which stood the tall, shapeless, solitary rock, frowning, like a shrouded giant, over the brawling of the small rivulet which watered the ravine." (See Pev. of Peak, Chap xvi). Some fragments of this huge stone were applied to the construction of the parsonage of St. Mark's.

Virgin Mary, "instituted the Cistercian discipline,
and made it a cell dependent on the abbey of Furness,
to which he gave not only the right of electing the
abbot of Rushen, but, as some say, the bishops of the
island.   It was a sort of Chapter to the Diocese.
Rushen Abbey was by king Olaf endowed with great
privileges and immunities.   Anno 1192 the monks removed to Douglas, but returned four years after.   In
the year 1257 Richard, Bishop of the isles, consecrated
the abbey church of St. Mary, Rushen, which (though
begun 130 years before and in that time had been
the repository of many of their kings,) it is probable
was not finished until that time.   This monastery
was in the year 1316 plundered by Richard de
Mandeville, who, with a numerous train of Irish,
landed at Ronaldsway on Ascension day and defeated
the Manxmen under Barrull mountain," (see Grose,
vol. vi, p. 205).   Bishop Ragnvald, who died in 1225;
King Olaf Gudrödson, who died at Peel Castle in
1237; Gospatrick, the celebrated Norwegian general
who died at Michael in 1240; King Ragnvald, who
was assassinated in 1248; King Magnus, who died
in 1265; and many other distinguished personages
were interred here.   In 1290 a "Letter of the men of
the Island of Man, who place themselves under the
protection of the King" (Edward I.) was written at
this abbey (see Rymer, t. ii., p. 492).   A copy of a
very curious indenture made here in 1508 may be
seen in Dr. Oliver's *Monumenta*, vol. iii., p. 25.

According to Tanner, Rushen Abbey flourished
some time after the suppression of religious houses
in England.   Grose remarks:—"Brown Willis, in
his History of Monasteries, says that anno 1553,
there remained in charge these following pensions.
To Henry Jackson, abbot, £10.   James More, John
Allowe, and Richard Novell, £1 : 13 : 4 each.
In the third year of the reign of King James, the
site of this abbey was in the Crown, where it had

remained ever since the dissolution, and was by that king leased to Sir Tho. Leighe, Knt. and Tho. Spencer, Esq., together with the Priory of Douglas, the Grey Friars at Brymaken, and the Rectories and Churches of Kirkcrist in Shelding, and Kirk Lavan, with their appurtenances, parcels of the Abbey of Rushen, usually lett at the annual rent of £101 : 15 : 11 for the term of 40 years at the same rent, and several other payments amounting to £21 : 17 : 0 as also a fine of £101 : 15 : 11 all woods, underwoods, mines, and quarries, being reserved to the Crown. This was excepted out of the grant made of the island afterwards by James I. to Henry, Earl of Northampton, and Robert, Earl of Salisbury; but afterwards granted anno 1611 [1609 ?] to William, Earl of Derby, and Elizabeth his wife, and their heirs, to hold of the Manor of East Greenwich, paying the accustomed rents; and afterwards confirmed by Act of Parliament, reserving the rights of Leighe and Spencer, the former lessees, during the term of their lease." It does not appear that an attempt was ever made to preserve this ancient abbey from decay. The principal parts now remaining are two ruinous square towers, and a small arched structure, which probably covers the entrance to a vault. To the antiquary, this ruin is rich in objects of the most interesting character. "In the abbey garden," says Dr. Neale, "is a' tombstone, which has given rise to the most absurd conjectures on the part of Manx antiquaries. It is a Dosd'ane, carved with a cross, and a sword by its side, evidently a knight's tomb." A splendid stone coffin, enriched with sculpture, a number of beautifully ornamented tiles—the remains of an ancient pavement—and various silver coins and rings have recently been discovered here. Human remains also have been found in abundance, including a cranium of enormous size. In 1851 a small coin bearing on the one side the words "HANS KRAVINKEL IN NAVR," and on the other the words "GOTES SEGEN MACHT REICH," *i.e.*, "God's blessing maketh rich," was discovered in this garden. A translation of this old German inscription was given by the present writer in *Mona's Herald* of September 3rd, 1851. In the immediate vicinity of the abbey is an ancient bridge called the Crossag; there are two arches. The passage over it is only about six feet broad. "The abbey bridge," says Dr. Neale, "would appear to be First-Pointed."

Quitting this interesting locality, we ascend the hill, and pursue the road which conducts to the parish church, an unpretending structure, dedicated to St. Lupus. The famous Illiam Dhone was interred in the chancel. A curious legend concerning the chalice will be found in Chapter XIII. The following inscription may be seen in the churchyard :— "Susanna Taubman, alias Quay, died July 2nd, 1784, aged 71. She was born on a Midsummer-day, married on a Midsummer-day, and buried on a Midsummer-day!" Leaving Malew Church, we proceed southward, and in a short time arrive at Castletown.

One of the most interesting objects in the vicinity of the metropolis of Man is the basaltic pile called the Stack of Scarlet, which is situate at the southwest extremity of Castletown Bay: geologists assert that it owes its formation to the operation of an ancient submarine volcano. "Stack" (stackr) is an Old Norse term. It signifies an insulated columnar rock which rises out of the sea. Adjacent to the Stack of Scarlet is what is called "Cromwell's Walk." Poolvash is at no great distance from it. At this place is a quarry of black marble: it possesses a sort of historical celebrity from having furnished the steps which ascend to the entrance of St. Paul's Cathedral, in London.

Entering *Arbory-street* from the market-place at

Castletown, and advancing westward, we pass a windmill standing on the left-hand side, and soon reach the parish of—

ARBORY. It is bounded on the north by Patrick, on the south by the sea, on the east by Malew, and on the west by Rushen. After proceeding about a mile and a half from Castletown, we approach Balladoole, which lies on the south side of the road. An old Treen chapel stands on this estate. A beautiful avenue of trees will be observed here. Turning to the left and entering it, we pass Balladoole House, and after a pleasant walk across the fields, arrive at the sea shore, where there is a salt spring which runs very rapidly. Not far from this spring, at a place called Strandhall, a submerged wood was discovered many years since: Dr. M'Culloch states that it was observed after a violent gale from the south, which, by removing the sand, disclosed the remains of a forest lying in a horizontal position, the trees having fallen towards the shore.

Retracing our steps to the high road, we pursue the first path on the right-hand side. It conducts to the ruins of the ancient Friary of Brymaken, or Bimaken, which was founded, according to Tanner, in 1373. Not far from the Friary stands the parish church, which was erected in 1757; it is dedicated to St. Columbus. The building is situate on high ground, and commands an extensive view of the surrounding country. A church stood upon the site of the present edifice in the thirteenth century. The register of the parish commences in 1670. Several remarkable stone circles may be seen in Arbory; many of the stones are of great size.

About a mile and a half from the church is Colby, an attractive little village: its romantic glen is well worthy of a visit.

Returning once more to the high road, from which

E

we have deviated, we again advance westward, and
enter the parish of—

RUSHEN, which is bounded by Arbory, Patrick,
and the sea. Kentraugh, the beautiful seat of E. M.
Gawne, Esq., Speaker of the House of Keys, will be
observed on the right-hand side; an extensive rabbit
warren may be seen on the left. Proceeding, we
soon arrive at—

PORT ST. MARY, a thriving fishing village, with a
good natural harbour: this village is said to derive its
name from an ancient Roman Catholic Chapel (called
St Mary's) which formerly stood adjacent to it. Not
far from it stand two tall and ponderous stones,
erected to the memory of some celebrated Scandinavian chieftains. Tradition states that they were
hurled hither from the summit of the Mull Hills by
two giants, in playing at quoits; and hence these
stones, which are about ten feet high, are called the
Giants' Quoiting Stones! The sail from Port St.
Mary to the Calf of Man, along the face of the stupendous cliffs of Spanish Head, will astonish and gratify
the lover of wild and romantic scenery. In that
lofty headland, it is said, there is a cavern of
immense extent, which is only accessible by boat, and
in favourable weather.

While he is in Port St. Mary, the visitor should
make an overland excursion to Spanish Head, near
which "the sections of the cliffs are vertical; and
as they attain an altitude of about three hundred
feet, they assume considerable grandeur of character.
Here a circumstance occurs of some interest to the
geological as to the general traveller. Large portions
of the land have been separated by vertical fissures,
extending from the surface almost to the level of the
shore beneath, so deep and so dark that the eyes does
not penetrate to the bottom. The principal masses
have thus slid into new positions, while many smaller

fragments appear suspended in the very act of falling; even the larger seeming to be often so nicely poised, that the hand would almost be thought sufficient to push them from their present situations into the sea that rolls below."

> " It is a fearful thing
> To stand upon the beetling verge and see
> Where storm and lightning from that huge gray wall,
> Have tumbled down vast blocks, and at the base
> Dashed them in fragments."

Those who have no taste for the wild beauties of nature should not come here; and the tourist who does not walk with fear over these tremendous CHASMS must at least walk with caution. Dr. Neale, speaking of Spanish Head, says:—"This cape, which is said to be so named from the loss of some vessels of the Armada, is a conglomeration of columns, heaped together in the wildest and most chaotic manner, with a fearful chasm rifting the precipice from top to bottom. With a good head you may clamber down one step after another of the graduated edge, and hear the clang of innumerable sea-fowl around you, the howling of the wind above you, and the booming of the sea in the rock-groined caverns below you. It is the grandest scene in the Isle of Man." Some convulsion of nature appears to have occurred here in far-off times of which alone geology takes cognizance.

> "There the screaming sea-bird flits,
>   Dips in the wave his dusky form,
> Or on a rocky turret sits,
>   The exulting demon of the storm."

A small stone circle—probably the burial-place of some distinguished Norwegian viking—may be seen in the immediate vicinity of the Chasms. Near Noggin Head is the lofty insulated rock designated the "Sugar-loaf." At no great distance, near the summit of the Mull Hills, is the lonely hamlet called

E 2

Craigneesh, a corruption of a Scandinavian appellation. This hamlet derives its name from the *nes* or
naze upon which it is situate. In the Lords' Book
the old name is written Crotnesse. Many of the inhabitants of Craigneesh are not able to converse in
English. From this wild locality the prospects are
inexpressibly grand and impressive. If the visitor
be so inclined, he may now proceed to—

PORT ERIN (frequently pronounced Iron), a charming little watering place greatly resorted to by
tourists. This pleasant fishing village possesses an
excellent natural harbour (about half a mile in
width, and a mile in depth inward), easy of access,
and affording shelter from north, south, and east
winds. On the completion of the breakwater now in
process of construction, vessels of large tonnage will
be enabled to ride here in safety during the preva-
lence of westerly gales. This district is famous for
its very bold and romantic coast-scenery. Brada
Head,* a stupendous pile of black rock, forms the
northern side of this delightful harbour: the southern
headland is called the Cassels. A large hotel, called
the Falcon's Nest, has recently been erected at Port
Erin by Mr. Milner, of Liverpool. St. Catherine's
Well, at this place, is celebrated for its medicinal
waters.

From Port Erin it is usual to make the passage to
the small island called the Calf,† always an object of
curiosity to visitors. We may state that the charge
made by the boatmen for conveying tourists to that
picturesque islet, is "ten shillings and a bottle of
rum!" The narrow and rocky channel which

---

* This huge metalliferous mass of rock was called by the
Northmen Bradhawe—*i.e.*, the broad head. In the name
Brada Head the use of the latter word is a redundancy.

† The name Calf was frequently given by the Northmen to
small islands in the neighbourhood of a larger one.

separates the Calf from the main island, with the
boisterous tide that runs through it, and the high
rocky shores that extend from Port Erin to Spanish
Head, present much interesting scenery to the
tourist. The—

CALF ISLAND is about five miles in circumference,
including an area of six hundred acres, part of which
is under cultivation. Its north-west coast is girt by
a broad belt of rent and dislocated rocks, tumbled
together in indescribable confusion, and by innumerable apertures of great depth, through which the
sea, when agitated by the violent gales from the
opposite quarter, rushes with tremendous impetu-
osity. The southern extremity rises into majestic
cliffs, about four hundred feet in height, on the top
of which stands the double lighthouse. According
to tradition, this solitary islet has been at different
times the retreat of two hermits. The first of these,
it is said, resided here in the reign of Queen
Elizabeth, as a penance for having murdered a beautiful woman in a fit of jealousy. The other, Thomas
Bushell, was Chancellor Bacon's amanuensis. His
motives for making this islet his abode are thus
explained by himself (see Wood's Account, &c., p.
144):—"The embrions of my mines proving abortive by the fall and death of Lord Chancellor Bacon,
were the motives which persuaded my pensive retire-
ment to a three years' solitude in the desolate isle,
called the Calf of Man, where, in obedience to my
dead Lord's philosophical advice, I resolved to make
a perfect experiment upon myself, for the obtaining
of a long and healthy life, most necessary for such
a repentance as my former debauchedness required,
by a parsimonious diet of herbs, oil, mustard, and
honey, with water sufficient, most like to that of our
long-lived fathers before the flood, as was conceived
by that Lord; which I most strictly observed, as if
obliged by a religious vow, till Divine Providence

called me to more active life." Mr. Montagu says:—
"It was the custom, in the time of Lord Bacon, for
young men of property to attach themselves, as
pages, to noblemen of eminence. It appears that
Mr. Bushel, who had large property at Eustone
[Enston ?], near Oxford, was, when he was fifteen
years old, admitted into the family of Lord Bacon,
and that he was under great obligation to him.
Bushel's words are—'his acceptance of me for his
servant at fifteen years of age upon my own address,
his clearing all my debts three several times with no
smaller sum in the whole than £3000, his preferring
me in marriage to a rich inheritrix, and thereupon
not only allowing me £400 per annum, but to
balance the consent of her father in the match,
promised upon his honour to make me the heir of
his knowledge in mineral philosophy.' Aubrey, in
his anecdotes, when describing the walks at Gorham-
bury, says—'Here his lordship much meditated, his
servant, Mr. Bushel, attending him with his pen and
ink-horn to set down present notions.' He was born
about 1602, and was therefore in 1620, at the time of
Lord Bacon's fall, about eighteen years old: and
about twenty-six, in 1626, when Lord Bacon died.
After the death of Lord Bacon, Bushel retired to the
Isle of Man, as he relates in his own work ... As
this tract was published in 1659, he was then near
sixty years of age, as is explained in part of the
tract, viz.—In the address to the reader, in the beginning of this tract, he says: 'But now seriously
considering that the taper of my life burns in the
socket (I having already numbered twelve lustres of
years)', and as by a lustre I understand five years, I
conclude therefore that Bushel was sixty years in
1659. Bushel always speaks of Lord Bacon in terms
of the most grateful respect ... 'He died at the age
of eighty in 1684. He lay sometime at Captain
Norton's, in the gate at Scotland Yard, where he

died seven years since (now 1684) about eighty ætat.
Buried in the little cloysters at Westminster Abbey,
somebody put B. B. upon the stone (now, 1787, all
new paved).'—Aubrey, 260 . . . 'Bushel was a very
strange man, and has told so many improbable
stories of his master and so many silly ones of himself, that what he says deserves no credit; further
than as it agrees with other evidence.'—Tennison's
Account of Lord Bacon's Works, p. 97."

What is called Bushell's house may still be seen;
it is situated upon the highest ground in the islet,
and within a few yards of a precipitous cliff. The
Calf is plentifully stocked with rabbits. Waldron
asserts that weapons of pure gold, and a large silver
crucifix, were discovered here at the commencement
of the eighteenth century. A slab on which is carved
a representation of the crucifixion was found here
many years since.

Several high columnar rocks surround this little
island. On the western side, two singular pillars of
a triangular shape, called the Stacks, rise to a considerable height above the ocean. The dangerous
rocks called the Chickens and the Burrough, may be
seen on the south side: near the summit of the latter
is an excavation in the form of a cross. The Eye, a
remarkable perforated rock about 100 feet high, is
not far distant. In the channel or sound that
separates the Calf from the main island, lies Kitterland which affords herbage to a few sheep in
summer.

On returning to Port Erin, we recommend the
tourist to explore the beauties of the neighbouring
country. Two miles to the north-east of the village
is the wild and romantic inlet called Fleshwick,
situate at the southern extremity of Ennyn-mooar.
The surrounding district is full of unfrequented and
unsuspected beauty. A road conducts from Fleshwick to Peel—a favourite resort of visitors; but as

we intend to approach that interesting old town by a
different route, we shall at present suspend our
researches in that direction.   Returning to Port
Erin we proceed eastward.   After a pleasant walk of
about three-quarters of a mile, we come to a point
where four roads meet.   Here formerly stood the
tallest monumental cross in the island; it is about
eight feet high.   This relic of antiquity may be seen
in an adjacent farmyard.   Pursuing the road branching to the left, we approach the parish church of
Rushen—an unpretending structure, adapted to hold
a congregation of four hundred and fifty persons.
The new parochial school-house in the vicinity of the
church is a handsome memorial to Captain Kermode,
a Manxman, who died a few years since in Tasmania.
Not far from the church, near Ballachurry,* may be
seen Cronk-Mooar, *i.e.*, the large hillock (called by
the inhabitants Fairy Hill) which deserves careful
examination.   This ancient fort is a truncated cone
about forty feet high, and about four hundred and
fifty feet in circumference at the base.   The summit
forms an area of twenty-five feet in diameter, surrounded by elevated edges about six feet high in the
form of a parapet.   At the base are the remains of a
deep and wide fosse.   An ancient Treen chapel stands
on the estate of Ballagawne in this parish.

Leaving Rushen church, and taking a north-
easterly direction, we pass the private residence
called Bell Abbey (in Arbory), and arrive at Colby,
whence, advancing eastward, we proceed to the village of Arbory.   Continuing our journey, we soon
pass the ancient church of Malew, and shortly afterwards reach Castletown.

---

* On the pillars of the entrance-gate at Ballachurry are two
immense cannon-balls, bearing the following inscription :—
"Fired into his Majesty's ship *Superb*, while passing the
Dardanelles, in 1806."

CHAPTER IX.

DESCRIPTION OF RAMSEY, AND THE PARISHES OF MAUGHOLD, LEZAYRE, BRIDE, ANDREAS, JURBY, AND BALLAUGH.

"I'll shew thee every fertile inch o' the island."

SHAKESPEARE.

"There
The sunshine in the happy glens is fair,
And by the sea, and in the brakes
The grass is cool, the sea-side air
Buoyant and fresh."

MATTHEW ARNOLD.

RAMSEY is charmingly situated at the mouth of the Sulby river, in a magnificent bay which sweeps round the north-eastern portion of the Isle of Man, from the promontory called Maughold Head to the Point of Ayre. It is justly esteemed for the salubrity of its atmosphere, and is a favourite resort for invalids. "The town is backed by successive ranges of high lands, culminating in the noble mountain of North Barrull, 1842 feet in height. Sundry ravines and glens run up from the sea-shore, and from the banks of the river Sulby, into these mountain ranges; and it is in the character and variety of these glens that one of the crowning charms of the island consists. Anything more perfectly and enchantingly beautiful than some of these haunts it is impossible to imagine. Every possible combination of rock, wood, and water is here. Bright rippling streams dance down from the mountain sides, over beds of boulder stones, covered in many parts with the richest mosses, with here and there a waterfall of surpassing beauty. The steep banks are finely timbered, and the profusion and variety of ferns, creepers, wild flowers, and plants innumerable, combine to render these glens

scenes of Elysian loveliness. Wandering in a state
of half-dreamy ecstasy through these haunts, one
ceases to wonder at the wide-spread faith in fairy
superstitions which has always distinguished the
Manx population, and which still holds its sway
largely amongst the people; for if fancy might be
permitted specially to select any particular nooks as
designed by nature for fairy land, it would certainly
be such spots as Ballure Glen, Elfin Glen, and others.
Happy the London artist who first finds his way to
these primeval sketching grounds. He will be the
envy and admiration of his brethren of the brush when
he first reveals the treasures he has gathered upon
the walls of our metropolitan exhibitions. Great will
be the enthusiasm of piscatorial enthusiasts when,
for the first time, they throw a fly into the quiet pools
and rapid gurgling eddies of the Sulby. Should our
glorious marine painter, E. W. Cooke, ever find his
way to Ramsey, we hardly know which would prove
the stronger attraction, the sands for his pencil, or
Ballure Glen with its treasures for his unrivalled
fernery." Ramsey, which is small and irregular,
derives a slight degree of importance from being the
seat of justice for the northern district of the island.
Some of the principal streets are wide and open;
many of the dwelling-houses and shops are convenient, well-built, spacious, and even elegant. Near
the centre of the town in Parliament-street, stands
the court-house, a neat structure, where the deemster,
the vicar-general, and the high-bailiff hold their
respective courts. A church dedicated to St. Paul
is situated on the south side of the market-place;
another, dedicated to St. Olave, stands in the Sandy-
road. The Wesleyan chapel, a handsome structure, is
in Waterloo-road. Near it is the Presbyterian Kirk.
The Roman Catholics have a small chapel here.
There are two excellent and well-conducted hotels,
the Albert and the Mitre. Near the pier stand the

premises of the steam-packet company. The harbour will admit vessels drawing seventeen or eighteen feet of water at spring tides, and eleven or twelve feet at neap tides. There is a stone pier which runs out a few hundred feet to sea, and is terminated by a lighthouse : Mr. Abernethy proposes to lengthen the north pier about 700 feet, curving it towards the south. The sands are almost unrivalled both for extent and beauty; and are so firm and level that they constitute the race-course on which the annual races are run.

> "The ocean old,
> Centuries old,
> Strong as youth, and as uncontroll'd,
> Paces restless to and fro,
> Up and down the sands of gold."

Ramsey, in a historical point of view, is one of the most celebrated towns in the island. Though it has a modern appearance, exhibiting but few vestiges of antiquity, there is reason to believe that its origin may be carried back to a very early date. About 1079 Gudröd Crovan, succeeded in conquering the Isle of Man after a battle at Scacafell, or Skyhill, near Ramsey, in which King Fingal, grandson of Sigtrygg, King of the Danes in Dublin, fell, as well as Sigtrygg Mac Olaf, the actual Danish King of Dublin. According to the "Chronicon Manniæ," "Gudröd Crovan assembled a multitude of ships, and arriving at Man, gave battle to the inhabitants, but was worsted and repulsed. Recruiting his forces and navy, he again came to Man, and engaging, was beat and put to flight. He once more got together a considerable army, and coming by night to the harbour called Ramsö, concealed three hundred men in a wood upon a declivity of the mountain Scacafell. At sunrise the Manx drew up their troops and attacked Gudröd with great fury. During the heat of

the engagement the three hundred men, issuing from
an ambuscade in the rear, galled the Manx and
obliged them to give ground.   The Manx, seeing
themselves overpowered, losing all hopes of a retreat,
as it was a full tide in the harbour of Ramsö, and the
enemy at their heels, with pitiful cries begged of
Gudröd to spare their lives.   He, moved with com-
passion, and commiserating the situation of a people
among whom he had been educated, called off his
forces and put an end to the pursuit.   On the following day Gudröd gave his troops the option of
dividing the Isle of Man among them for an inheritance, or of pillaging it and returning home.   They
chose to plunder the country, to enrich themselves
with the booty, and then retire.   Gudröd, however,
distributed to such of the islanders as remained with
him the southern part of the island, and the northern
division to the natives, on condition that no one
whatever should attempt the establishment of a
hereditary claim to any part of the island."   In 1154
King Olaf, surnamed Bitlingr, or Klining, was
assassinated near Ramsey haven.   In 1156 a sea
battle was fought in Ramsey Bay between the fleets
of Gudröd and Somerled, with great slaughter on
both sides.   In 1645 a band of Scotch pirates landed
here and plundered the town.   Fort Loyal was soon
afterwards built by the Earl of Derby to protect
Ramsey from foreign enemies; no vestige of this
fortification now remains.   In 1651 the transports
with the Parliamentary forces under Colonel Duckenfield anchored in this bay : a deputation, consisting
of John Christian, Ewan Curphey, and William
Standish, went on board to negotiate for the surrender of the isle, the only stipulation made on the
part of the Manx being that they might enjoy their
lands and liberties as they formerly had.   On the
21st of October, 1688, William, Prince of Orange,

afterwards King of England, was nearly wrecked on a sand-bank near the entrance of Ramsey Bay : from that circumstance the bank has since been called King William's Bank. A naval engagement took place on the 28th of February, 1760, near the northern coasts of Man, between the squadron commanded by the celebrated Thurot and that commanded by Captain Elliot. "They were exactly three frigates to three. The French ships were much the larger, and their men much more numerous ; but both ships and men were in a bad condition. A sharp and close engagement begun. None of the French could possibly escape, and they must take or be taken. Thurot did all that could be expected from the intrepidity of his character; he fought his ship until she had her hold almost filled with water, and her decks covered with dead bodies. At length he was killed. The crew of his ship, and by her example those of the other two, dispirited by this blow, and pressed with uncommon alacrity by the signal bravery of Captain Elliot, and those who commanded under him, struck, and were carried into Ramsey Bay in the Isle of Man. Even this inconsiderable action added to the glory of the English arms " (see Annual Reg., vol. iii., p. 57). To commemorate the defeat of Thurot, Mark Hildesley, Bishop of Sodor and Man, erected a monument in the immediate neighbourhood of the episcopal palace.

About a mile from Ramsey (on the Douglas road), embosomed in trees at the foot of the mountain ranges, stands an old chapel. It was consecrated in 1753 by Bishop Wilson. This structure is built upon the site of an ancient Roman Catholic church. A little further on, near Ballure-bridge, is a delightful walk along the umbrageous glen of Claughbane. A pleasant path conducts through the plantations to the summit of the hill on which stands ALBERT TOWER.

This elegant and substantial structure is erected on the spot where the late Prince Consort stood on the 20th of September, 1847 ; it was built in 1848 to commemorate the royal visit. The prospect from the battlements of this tower is magnificent, embracing the northern district of the island—

> "Hill, dale, and shady woods, and sunny plains,
> And liquid lapse of murmuring streams"—

the capacious bay of Ramsey, the mountains of Cumberland, and the coasts of Scotland.

Returning to Ballure-bridge, we take a south-easterly direction, leaving the lofty mountain called North Barrull on the right-hand, and soon reach the shore road, pursuing which we pass the villas of Folieu, Belle Vue, and Lewaigue, and reach the charming coves called Port Lewaigue and Port-le-Voillen. Near the latter, on the left-hand side of the road, stands an old cross, about five feet high, on which there are five bosses. Proceeding we soon arrive at the village of MAUGHOLD, which, although now sunk into insignificance, is of high antiquity. It was formerly more populous than Ramsey, which circumstance may be attributed to the resort of pilgrims to the famous shrine of St. Maughold, or rather Maccaille. That saint was constituted bishop of the isle about the end of the fifth century, and died in 518. It is alleged that he was originally captain of a gang of Irish banditti. The parish church, a neat structure, seventy-two feet long and seventeen broad, dedicated to the renowned saint above-mentioned, is celebrated for its ancient monuments. "The chancel," says Dr. Neale, "is First-Pointed. There has been an eastern triplet, but the central light has been taken out, and a three-light Third-Pointed-window inserted in its place. These lights are cinq-foiled, the window being almost square-headed, and form the only foliations now remaining in the island. On the north side of the chancel have been two lancets. The second is now Debased. On the south side, towards the east end, is a lychnoscope, of which the upper part is blocked, thereby differing in two particulars from its sister windows in England. In the nave, on the north, the windows have been altered—on the south there were five lancets. The font, which is scandalously placed outside, at the west end, a circular bason without stem, seems of the same date. The western porch is Romanesque, shallow and waggon-vaulted from two square rude piers: the edge of the waggon-vaulting worked into a kind of nail-head." The church is surrounded by an extensive cemetery. "In it," says the same authority, "are two more crosses, one a plain wheel cross, vertical, and three feet and a half in height, at the south of the church: the other near its west end, flat, and with a wheel at each end." Two ancient crosses, discovered a few years since on removing some stone steps, have been set up against the wall near the porch. "On the lower part of one of these stones," says the Rev. W. Kermode, "on each side of the cross, are two monkish figures seated, the chair being distinctly traceable in the case of one; whence we conclude they were intended for two bishops—probably St. Patrick and St. Maughold. Underneath these figures on either side, is what appears to be a man on horse-back." Runic characters are said to be traceable on the inner edge of the lintel over the west door of the church. Fragments of other crosses, and a stone bearing the figure of an animal resembling the elk, were also found here. Another beautiful cross, elaborately ornamented on both sides, stands near the south side of the gate of the churchyard. At the north side of the gate may be seen an elegant pillar cross—" a Third-Pointed erection, very perfect and beautiful. It is raised on four [three] square

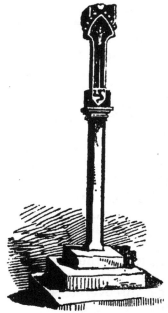

steps—the stem is octagonal; the capital is adorned with four shields—one, the arms of Man—one, a mere wheel tracery, the other two much effaced.   From this springs the real rood, bearing on its four sides our crucified Lord, our Lady and the Divine Infant,—S. Bridget kneeling, perhaps about to take the veil, and S. Maughold." The parish register begins in 1647.   On the bold mossy promontory designated Maughold Head, not far from the church, is St. Maughold's Well; the water is celebrated for its medicinal properties. Adjacent to the spring is the saint's chair.   Pursuing the road conducting from the parish church to Cornah, we come to the beautiful waterfall of Ballaglass. This splendid cascade—

> " Down flowing from its dizzening height,
>   One dazzling gush of liquid light,"

is formed by the Dhoon rivulet, which flows into the picturesque creek called Cornah.   The lovely waterfall, and the charming scenery in the midst of which it is situate, deservedly attract much attention.   In this locality, on the summit of a hill, stands a large stone circle; the natives call it Castle Chorry.   Not far distant is the old burial-ground of the Quakers. It is termed Ruillick ny Quakeryn, *i.e.*, the graveyard of the Quakers.   A few of the followers of Penn seem to have lived in the parish about two centuries ago.   The religious society of St. Bee's in Cumberland, formerly possessed some valuable property in

Maughold. On the estate of Ballacannell, about a mile and a half from the church, may be seen the ruins of an ancient chapel, and a remarkable old monumental cross four feet long and eighteen inches wide. The arms of the cross are decorated with ornaments of the intertwined pattern; below is a singular representation of what seems to be a human figure.

While he is in this quarter, the visitor ought to ascend the noble conical mountain North Barrull.* Those who climb its summit, which is 1842 feet above the level of the sea, are rewarded with a splendid and extensive prospect. Ramsey and its beautiful bay lie at the foot of the mountain; the level and highly cultivated northern plateau of the island stretches away almost down to Peel Castle in the west. Far away in the east, through the blue haze of the sea, rise the lofty mountains of Cumberland, and still off towards the north, some of the Scottish hills bound the horizon, whilst westward the Irish coast trends away till lost in the distance. The view along the mountain ranges of the interior of the island, as seen from the summit of North Barrull, is very fine; and high above the numerous summits towers the magnificent peak of Snaefell, the highest mountain on the island.

Retracing our steps to Ramsey, we enter Parliament-street, and after proceeding a short distance, reach the parish of

LEZAYRE. On the left-hand side, at the foot of Sky-hill (renowned for the battles that were fought in its vicinity during the early periods of Manx history), is seen Milntown, a beautiful castellated edifice. The romantic Glen Aldyn, through which a

---

* Barrull literally signifies the "Big Peak." The name is composed of the Irish words *Bar*, a point, the head or top of a thing—and *ull* (pronounced ool), great or big.

mountain stream courses its way, adding its tribute
to the Sulby river, is immediately in the rear. The
road which branches to the left at Milntown conducts
through Glen Aldyn to Snaefell.

In former times several lakes existed in the northern
district of the isle. One of these, named Mirescoge,*
was near the base of the mountains. In Johnstone's
Antiquitates Celto-Normannicæ, mention is made of
three islets in it, on one of which, it is affirmed, a
miracle was once performed! See chap. xiii. In 1505
a grant of one moiety of the fishery in Mirescoge was
made by Thomas, Earl of Derby, to Huan Hesketh,
bishop of the island.

Advancing westward through a richly cultivated
and beautifully wooded country, we approach the
parish church, an edifice of much architectural merit,
dedicated to the Holy Trinity.   It is charmingly

situated at the base of a mountain, and is embosomed
in stately trees. The parish register commences in

† "Mirescoge *alias* Ballamona.—A monastery was built here
A.D. 1176 by the abbot Sylvanus, who had land given him for
it by Godred, King of Man.   But it was afterwards granted to
the abbey of Russin, and the monks removed thither."—Tanner's
Notitia Monastica., p. 722.

1636. Continuing our journey, we reach Sulby bridge, which is about four and a half miles from Ramsey. Near this bridge is Cronk Samark, *i.e.*, Shamrock Hill, a towering, fantastically-shaped rock, situate at the entrance of Sulby Glen; from its summit a beautiful and extensive prospect is obtained. According to Dr. Paterson, we have here a very early specimen of a hill-fort. We soon come to a road (branching to the left,) that conducts to the romantic

glen of Sulby, where may be seen a fine cascade which issues through a remarkable natural bridge. The scenery of this ravine invariably calls forth the admiration of visitors, and will amply repay a long journey. The path is cut along the base of the mountain on the right-hand side of the glen; now it winds by a precipice, with scarcely half a foot of spare room for a carriage to pass, and anon, it descends to the brink of the rivulet which glides through this picturesque vale. This stream is the largest in the island, and affords good sport to anglers. As we proceed, the scenery assumes a more savage and desolate appearance, and the ravine narrows in as we approach the base of Snaefell. The tourist should ascend this noble mountain, on gaining the summit of which he will be repaid by his labour by the most extensive and magnificent prospects.

Returning once more to Ramsey, we cross the substantial stone bridge of three arches, that spans the Sulby river, and advance northward along the *Sandy-road*. A church dedicated to St. Olave will be observed on the right-hand side. Proceeding, we

pass a remarkable mound called Cronk Aust, which
stands on the west side of the road. Continuing our
journey, we soon enter the parish of

BRIDE, which is bounded on the north and east by
the sea, on the south by Lezayre, and on the west by
Andreas. Point Cranstal, in this parish, was anciently
called Shellack Poynt (see Blome's *Britannia*).
Most of this headland has been swept away by the
sea. In this locality is Cronk-ny-Vowlan, an ancient
sepulchral mound surrounded with stones. The
parish church, an unpretending structure, is dedicated
to St. Bridget; it overlooks the Point of Ayre, and
commands a view of the extensive bay of Ramsey.
The living is a rectory in the gift of the Crown. The
late Miss Nelson, authoress of "Island Minstrelsy,"
resided at the rectory. Opposite the gate of the
church-yard may be seen a remarkable old cross.
Some years since an old battle-axe was dug up on
the estate called Kimeragh in this parish. Speaking
of the census of 1861, a facetious writer remarks:
"Bride is the only parish out of the seventeen into
which the island is divided, in which every Jockey
could not get his Jenny. It might have been
supposed that the parish of Bride would have supplied
brides for all the male population in the district if all
had been matrimonially disposed, but the fact is
otherwise, there being in Bride fewer females than
males. This state of things having been pointed out,
perhaps there will be an immigration into Bride of
eligible brides from the other overstocked parishes in
the island." The POINT of Ayre (from *öre* or *eyri*,
the old Scandinavian name for the sandy point of a
promontory), an extensive waste, chiefly of sand-hills,
is about seven miles from Ramsey, and sixteen from
Burrow Head in Scotland; this is the northern
extremity of the Isle of Man. From it a sandy beach
extends to Ramsey, and almost to Peel. On the
point stands a lighthouse one hundred and six feet

high. [Leaving the parish church of Bride, and taking [a south-westerly direction, we enter the parish of

ANDREAS, which is bounded on the north by the sea, on the south by Lezayre, on the east by Bride, and on the west by Jurby. At the north of this parish may be seen the Lhane, where, according to tradition, a celebrated King of Man, vulgarly called Orry, landed, in the tenth century (see Chapter II.) In former times a lake of large dimensions fell into the sea near this place. Not far distant are Cronk-narrai-shage, *i.e.*, the hill of the watch by day, and the remarkable sepulchral mound designated Cronk-ny-Dooinney. The parish church is dedicated to St. Andrew. The living, a rectory in the gift of the Crown, has generally been held by the archdeacons of the island. It is said that the marble font once belonged to Philip I. of France. In the centre of the green, near the gate of the church, stands a mutilated fragment of a beautiful Runic cross. The inscription, which is nearly obliterated, runs thus :

"....THANA AF UFAIG FAUTHUR SIN IN GAUTR GIRTHE SUNR BIARNAR."

i.e., "(N. N. erected) this (cross) to his father Ufeig, but Gaut Björnson made it." See inscription No. 16, Chapter VI., and also Worsaae's "Danes and Northmen," p. 284. In the churchyard may be seen an extremely well-preserved monumental cross (represented in the annexed engraving), on which are carved scrolls, birds, horses, swine, a stag, &c. It bears the following Runic inscription :

"SANDULF EIN SUARTI RAISTI KRUS THANA AFTIR ARIN BIAURG KUINU SINA."

i.e., "Sandulf the Swarthy erected this cross to his wife Arnbjörg." See inscription No. 14, Chapter VI., and also Worsaae, p. 281. The church register begins in

1666. Near the church is a mound called Cronk
Ballavarry. At Ballachurry there is a fine old
fortified camp, the erection of which is ascribed by
Chaloner to the seventh Earl of Derby, who was
decapitated in 1651. It is thus described by Colonel
Townley: "It is more complete than any I have
seen in England of that time; the situation of it is
most eligible, being formed on a small natural
eminence in a very level district. The internal square
on which the troops encamped, is a level piece of
ground, sunk so much below the bastions and curtains
as effectually to secure the troops within from any
attack of fire-arms without; this space is one hundred
and fifty feet long, and one hundred and twenty feet
broad; the fosse is twenty feet wide, and the outer
rampart is twelve feet high. There are four noble
bastions, one at each corner, sixty feet in diameter.
There is no breach in any part of the works, which
favours the supposition that the troops retained
peaceable possession of their fortified camp." Not
far from Ballachurry is a handsome chapel of ease,
dedicated to St. Jude. We now proceed to describe
the parish of

JURBY, which is bounded by the sea, Andreas,
Lezayre, and Ballaugh. In former times the principal
place in the parish appears to have been called
Ivarsby, i.e., Ivar's town or village. That appellation
has probably been corrupted into Jurby. The point
of land bearing that name forms the north-western
extremity of the island: on it may be seen the ancient
watch-hill designated Cronk-mooar. The curragh
drain intersects the parish. In the peat are
frequently found immense trunks of oak and fir.
The church is dedicated to St. Patrick. It is situated
on an eminence about a quarter of a mile from Jurby
Point, and commands an extensive prospect of the
sea and of the opposite coast. A church stood near
the site of the present edifice in the thirteenth century.

In the garden of the vicarage is a fragment of a very beautiful Runic cross. The inscription, which is imperfect, runs thus:

"... RU SUN IN ANAN RAITI FAIRTHUR JAL. .."

Professor Munch remarks upon this inscription: "RAITI is mis-spelled for RAISTI; FAIRTHUR is rather curious; I have ventured to suggest the form FAETHÓRR, which may be called grammatically possible, but never occurs anywhere in books or monuments. Perhaps the name is a Gaelic one, as Ferteth, Ferchad, only altered or misspelled. In Latin: ...*rae filium, sed aliam (crucem) erexit Fairthurus Jal.* .." See inscription No. 12, Chapter VI. Another Runic cross may be seen in a Treen chapel at West Nappin. Leaving Jurby, and proceeding southward, we come to the parish of

BALLAUGH, which is bounded on the north by Jurby, on the south by Michael and Braddan, on the east by Lezayre, and on the west by the sea. It derives its name from the Manx *Balla*, a town, or an estate, and *Logh*, a pool or a lake. A large lake called Balla-lough, which communicated with the sea at Ballamona-mooar, formerly existed here. To this lake, which has long since disappeared, the parish is unquestionably indebted for its name. Skeletons of the great fossil elk *(Megaceros Hibernicus)* have been found in Ballaugh. A splendid specimen of that extinct animal, discovered on the estate called Ballacain, is now in the museum of the University of Edinburgh. An engraving of it will be found in Chapter V.

The old parish church is about a mile and a half from Ballaugh village. In the churchyard stands a remarkably beautiful Runic cross; the inscription, which has been defaced by time, runs thus:

"THORLIBR THIUTULB SUNR R(AISTI) (KR)US THANA AFT(IR) (U)LB SUN SIN."

i.e., "Thorlaf Thjodolfson erected this cross to his son Ulf." See inscription No. 13, Chapter VI.

The new church, according to Dr. Neale, is remarkable for nothing but its ugliness. It was

erected in 1832, chiefly by money collected in England. The living is a rectory in the gift of the Crown. The church register, the oldest in the island, commences in 1598. While he is in this quarter, the tourist ought to visit the lovely vales called Ravensdale and Druidale.

Leaving Ballaugh, and taking a north-easterly direction, we return to Sulby bridge; whence, pursuing an eastward course, we soon reach our original starting-place, Ramsey.

CHAPTER X.

DESCRIPTION OF PEEL, AND OF THE PARISHES OF
PATRICK, GERMAN, AND MICHAEL.

"Hast thou seen that lordly castle,
    That castle by the sea ?
Golden and red above it
The clouds float gorgeously."

LONGFELLOW.

PEEL, anciently called Holm Town* and Halland
Town, and in Manx Purt-ny-Hinshey, *i.e.*, Harbour
of the Island is a place of considerable antiquity.
The name is derived from the Keltic *pil*, a strong-
hold or fortification.   What most interests the
traveller in this town is its noble castle, which is
situated on a rocky islet or *holm* called St. Patrick's
Isle, at the north-east termination of Peel Hill.
"The rock on which the Castle stands," says Dr.
Neale, "is most deeply interesting, and in the most
romantic situation conceivable.   It is now connected
with the island by a wall; but you have to be ferried
across.   The walls, erected in 1500, and enclosing a
space of about five acres, are tolerably perfect.   You
land at a curious flight of steps on the east; and in
the guard-room which you first enter are shown the
passage by which the Moddey Doo, the spectre hound,
used to enter [see Chapter XIII] .... To the east of
of the guard-room is the cathedral church of St.
Germanus, founded by Bishop Simon in 1245.   In
its general contour, and in the red sandstone which
forms its material, it is strikingly like Carlisle Cathedral, while the chancel much resembles S. Begh's.
The east wall rests absolutely on the edge of the pre-

---

* The Scandinavian term *holm* signifies a small island.

cipice. It is a small cross church with central tower, but without aisles or porches. The walls are perfect but unroofed; and the red sandstone of which they are composed, is so extremely friable, more especially where exposed to the fury of the north-west storms, here perfectly terrific, that it cannot stand much longer. Indeed the wonder is that the nave arch holds together as it is. The east window is a small, plain, unequal triplet, with interior drip-stone. On the north side of the chancel are five lancets, also quite plain; under them two arched recesses, covered with the mould, which has much risen; but probably the tomb of bishops. The arrangement of the south side is the same as that of the north, except. that under the fourth light is a door, leading down by a passage concealed in the thickness of the wall to a crypt, barrel-vaulted, and diagonal-ribbed from thirteen short shafts; but filled up to the spring of the arches with rubbish. Here Eleanor, Duchess of Gloucester,* is said to have been confined in 1440:

---

* Keightley, in his "History of England," says :—"About two years after, the Duchess of Gloucester was accused of treason and sorcery. The charge was that with the aid of Roger Bolingbroke, one of the Duke's chaplains, who was said to deal in the black art, and Margery Jourdemain, the witch of Eye, she had made a waxen image of the king, to whom the Duke was next heir, which was exposed to a gentle heat, for, according to the rules of magic, as it melted away, the king's health and strength would decline. She owned to having directed Bolingbroke to calculate the duration of the king's life. The result was that Bolingbroke was found guilty of treason and executed; the witch was burnt; the Duchess, after being made to walk three several times through the city without a hood, and bearing a lighted taper, was consigned for life to the custody of Sir John Stanley [in reality, Sir *Thomas* Stanley] in the Isle of Man."

The Duchess is referred to by Shakespeare in his play of "Henry VI." :—

"*King Henry.*—Stand forth, Dame Eleanor Cobham, Glo'ster's
    In sight of God and us your guilt is great;   [wife,

and to have lived for fourteen years: and I should add that, according to the castle tradition, the Moddey Doo is believed to have been her restless spirit. The arches which support the tower are somewhat later than the choir: they are of two orders, and seem early Middle-Pointed; but the sandstone is so much worn, that is impossible to speak certainly. The east window of the north transept was Middle-Pointed, and seems to have had two lights. The north is the same, except that it has a plain door beneath it. The west is a lancet. The east window of the south transept resembles that of the north, except that it

---

Receive the sentence of the law, for sins
Such as by God's book are adjudg'd to death.
You, madam, for you are more nobly born,
Despoiled of your honour in your life,
Shall after three day's open penance done,
Live in your country here in banishment
With Sir John Stanley, in the Isle of Man.

Duchess.—Welcome is banishment, welcome were my death, &c.

In Middleton's Legend of Humphrey, Duke of Gloucester (printed in 1600), we find the following :—

"They charge her that she did maintaine and feede
  Soul-killing witches, and convers'd with devils;
  Had conference with sprits, who should succeede
  The King; and by their meanes had wrought some evil
  Against his royall person; and had sought
  To end his life, and bring the state to nought.

  Upon surmises thus she was arraygn'd
  Witnes suborn'd and she condemn'd for it;
  And from her husband closely is detain'd;
  And that their doings might succeed, more fit
  To their desires, it is 'mongst them thought meete,
  She should doe open pennance in the streete;

  And, after that perform'd, be banisht hence
  Into the Isle of Man; and there should live
  A guiltless exile, for a small offence
  Or none at all; and who so ere did give
  That unjust sentence, hath ere this his doome
  Amongst th' condemn'd, where comfort nere shall come."

is not in the centre of that side, but more to the south. The south window is the same also, only it has no door under it, and is not in the middle, but to the east: above it in the gable is a small window of two lights. The west side has a lancet, and a door which, as leading up from the sea steps, was the principal entrance to the cathedral. On the left hand, inside, is a circular benatura. The nave was also Middle-Pointed. It has two blocked windows on the north, on the south four arches of construction, perhaps intended for a contemplated aisle, with four two-light obtuse-headed windows in them; the tracery has quite perished. The tower is short and squat, with a square belfry turret at its south-west angle. A heavy corbel table runs round the transepts . . . . In the enclosure of the castle walls is a small building, said to have been a church, and to have been under the invocation of S. Patrick. I say said to have been, because the structure is so exactly like what is said to have been the armoury, that it is difficult to believe one to have been an ecclesiastical, the other a profane building. As to its date, the only clue left is the excessive rudeness of its masonry." The Rev. Mr. Petit says:—"On the highest part of the island, not far from its centre, stands a round tower, of the same character with those peculiar to Ireland. Like them it has a door at some distance from the ground, and wider at the bottom than at the spring of the arch. There are also four square-headed openings near the top, and another lower down. The material of this tower is principally red sand-stone, laid in pretty regular courses of thin but long or wide blocks; the jointing is wide, and filled with a hard coarse mortar, which has been less acted upon by the atmosphere than the stone itself. The door faces the east, and the top window the cardinal points, according to the orientation of the cathedral. We have in England two striking examples of the combination of military and ecclesiastical structures, Porchester and Dover . . . Peel Castle and Cathedral offer a similar instance. That the little Isle of St. Patrick was devoted to purely ecclesiastical purposes, at the time of the first introduction of Christianity into the Isle of Man, is not impossible; but its position was too important to allow it to remain long unoccupied as a military station . . . The tower and other parts of the castle about the entrance, which is south of the cathedral, seem to belong to the early part of the fourteenth century; the masonry is strong and careful, though not very regular, and the blocks of stone larger than those used in other parts of the building. From the difficulty of access, this part must have been very defensible before the general use of artillery. The rest of the wall is of much later date." In the southern wall of the nave of the cathedral is a fragment of a monumental cross, with the following Runic inscription:—

" . . . (KR)US THENA EFTIR ASRITHI KUNU SINA DUTUR UTR,"

i.e., "(A. B. erected) this cross to his wife Asrid [Osred?], daughter of Ottar." This inscription is imperfect: the first part of it "A. B. raisti kr" was engraved on the fragment which has been lost. See inscription No. 6, Chapter VI.

A remarkable square pyramidical mound may be seen a little to the northward of the cathedral: each of its sides measures about seventy yards, and faces one of the cardinal points of the compass. Not far from this are the ruins of the so-called palaces of the Stanleys, and of the bishops of Sodor and Man.

Olaf, King of Man, died in Peel Castle in 1237. Thomas, Earl of Warwick was imprisoned here in 1397. Many of the early bishops of the island were interred in the cathedral. In 1844, a brass plate, which was supposed to have been stolen from bishop

Rutter's tomb, was discovered in the wall near the
sally-port of the castle. The following is the inscription on this curious relic, which is now at Bishop's
Court :—

> In hac domo, quam a vermiculis
> Mutuo accepi confratribus meis
> Sub spe Resurrectionis ad vitam,
> Jaceo Saml. permissione divina
> Episcopus hujus insulae. Siste, Lector,
> Vide ac ride, palatium Episcopi!
> Obt. 30mo die mensis Maii 1663.

Outside the walls of the castle is what is called the
giant's grave, a green mound about thirty yards in
length and one and a half in breadth. This giant
lived, according to tradition, contemporary with St.
Patrick, and, by his strength and ferocity, became the
terror of the island. He had three legs, and deemed
it the merest trifle in the world to transport himself
across the gorge between Peel Castle and Contrary
Head, at only one step. On a time, either for amuse-
ment, or in a fit of rage, he lifted a large block of
white stone from the castle rock, and, though several
tons in weight, tossed it with the greatest ease
against the acclivity of one of the opposite hills, about
three miles distant, where the violence of its fall
broke it into three pieces, and where it is still visible
from the castle to this day : in this stone may be
seen what are called "the very marks of the giant's
fingers, which he crushed into it when he tossed it
from his hand." The giant, it appears, was soon
after taken to task for his wickedness by St. Patrick,
and, having attempted to kill the saint, was cursed
by him in the name of the Virgin, and forced to fly
out of the island : he rushed at one stride over Contrary Head, and was never since beheld in Man !
Before Government purchased the Royalty of this
place, the fortress was garrisoned by troops kept in
pay by the Lord of the Isle. This relic of past ages

is fast falling to decay; but we hope that some steps may be taken in time to preserve a structure to which so many historical recollections are attached. We conclude our description of Peel Castle with the following exquisitely beautiful lines, by G. H. Wood, Esq. :—

There is not a spot in Mona's Isle
   Has purer charms for me,
Than yonder lonely mouldering pile,
Which beams in the bright sun's parting smile,
   Ere he sinks in the western sea.
'Tis a hallow'd spot, with its turrets of light
   That gleam in the glassy wave,
Where its image is mirror'd so calm and bright,
You would think it the work of enchanter's might,
   Raised up from the ocean's grave.

There beams each hoary time-worn tower,
   All bent with the weight of years,
Like goodly Age in his dying hour,
Whilst sunny Hope's triumphant power
   Dispels his doubts and fears.
There stands the holy, mouldering fane,
   Where rest the sleeping dead,
Where they for ages long have lain,
And slept the sleep that knows no pain,
   Each in his grassy bed!

But roofless now is that holy pile,
   And its arches rent and riven;
Yet, I love to tread its lonely aisle;
Where the foot-fall only is heard the while,
   And muse on the things of heaven;
For who could cherish dark thoughts of gloom
   In a scene so bright and fair,
Where the sunbeams lighten the place of the tomb,
And gild the wild flowers that around us bloom,
   Which offer their incense there.

But let us explore the ruins around,
   And the Castle's lone dungeon cells,
Where the royal lady lay fettered and bound,
(Till lingering death her fetters unwound,)
   Accus'd of dark magic spells;

And the room near the dim portcullis door,
  Where the night watch oft was scar'd
By the "Spectre-Hound," so famed of yore,
As told in his Lay of Minstrel lore,
  By Scotia's brightest bard.

Then haste from these scenes of doubt and dread
  On the battlement's heights to roam,—
And gaze on the ocean's tranquil bed,
Where the sunset's purple hues are shed,
  Unruffled by the billow's foam;
Where the little pinnace, with white sails furl'd,
  Seems asleep in the calm sea's breast,
When not a breath the waves has curled,—
One lonely speck on the watery world,—
  Like a living thing at rest!

And watch the sun's declining ray,
  As we sit on the grassy mound,
Until the sweet hour when twilight grey,
Casts her dim mantle o'er tower and bay,
  And the ruined heaps around;—
And the lengthening shadows begin to fall,
  And the lone bat wings his flight;
And the dismal owl begins to call,
And hoot to his mate from the Castle wall,
  Deep hid in the dim twilight.

Then muse on the years long past awáy,
  When these walls echoed with glee,
On gallant knights and ladies gay,
Sweet minstrel's harp and roundelay,
  And feasts of chivalry.
And lingering still, till the lamp of night
  Is sparkling o'er the deep,—
And holy fane, and turret height
Seem slumbering in the pale moon-light
  In a calm and silvery sleep.

The town of Peel, which is in the parish of German,
consists of narrow and irregular streets, and stands
at the estuary of the Neb or the Great River, which
rises in the mountains of Michael. In the fishing
season the harbour is one of the principal resorts of
the herring fleets. The parish church is dedicated

to St. Peter. A Grammar School was founded here
in 1746, and a Mathematical School in 1763. Peel
has two excellent hotels, namely the Peel Castle
Hotel and the Marine Hotel. At the northern
boundary of Peel Bay there are several very grotesque and romantic caverns: the environs of the
town are picturesque and agreeable.

Advancing southward, we enter the parish of—

PATRICK, which is bounded on the north by German
and the sea; on the south by Rushen and Malew;
on the east by Malew and Marown; and on the west
by the sea. Kirk Patrick, which was consecrated

in 1715 by Bishop Wilson, stands at a short distance
from the town of Peel; the living is a vicarage in the
gift of the Bishop of the Isle. Until 1714 Patrick
was united to St. German's. In this parish, at a
distance of about a mile and a half from the church,
is the celebrated GLEN MEAY. It is a deep and rocky
glen, well wooded, through which runs a rivulet,
murmuring over its stony bed, and in one part forming a delightful fall of from thirty to forty feet. The
northern bank is almost perpendicular, covered with
luxuriant ivy intermixed with holly. The south side
exhibits a rich plantation of ash, chesnut, and hazel.

F

As the valley winds considerably, all foreign objects
are excluded, and the whole has an air of the most
pleasing solitude.   A little rustic wooden bridge
spans the waterfall.   Thousands of tourists flock
hither annually, and are enchanted with the beauty
and picturesqueness of this romantic locality.

About a mile from this charming spot (in Glen

Rushen) are the extensive quarries of the Manx Slate Company, which will well repay a visit.

Proceeding about two miles to the south, we come to—

DALBY, *i.e.*, the village in the dale, where there is a small chapel-of-ease, dedicated to St. James. There are several curious caves at the Niarbyl, or Dalby Point. Near the base of the lofty Cronk-na-Irey-Laa (*i.e.*, hill of the rising day), may be seen the so-called burial ground of the ancient kings of Man. That mountain rises to the height of 1445 feet : some Manx scholars are of opinion that its name is Cronk-yn-arrey-laa, *i.e.*, the hill of the watch by day. The picturesque attractions of this district are unsurpassed in any part of the Isle of Man. Advancing southward, we pass the glen designated the Lhag—obtaining a fine view of Dalby Point—and arrive at the north-western acclivity of South Barrull. At this point several roads meet : the famous Round Table, from which the views are superb, is adjacent. We would recommend all visitors to ascend South Barrull, whose breezy summit (1584 feet above the level of the sea) commands magnificent and extensive prospects.

FOXDALE MINES are not far distant. Upwards of one hundred tons of lead (each ton containing from fifty to sixty ounces of silver) are obtained per month. The depth of these mines is about two hundred fathoms. Upwards of five hundred workmen are employed here. At Foxdale there are a small chapel-of-ease, a Wesleyan chapel, and a news-room and library. This locality is by no means devoid of attractions to the tourist. Near Hamilton Bridge may be seen a very beautiful cascade. Slieau Whuaillan (*i.e.*, the mountain of the whelp), on the western side of this romantic vale, rises to the height of 1086 feet. Tradition says that in days of yore persons suspected of witchcraft were taken to its summit, and after having been placed in a barrel with

F 2

sharp iron spikes inserted round the interior, were
rolled down the northern declivity of the mountain!

We now proceed to describe the parish of—

GERMAN, which extends about six and a half miles
from north to south, and about four from east to
west, and is bounded on the north by Michael, on the
south by Marown and Patrick, on the east by
Marown, and on the west by the sea.

The chief object of interest in this parish is
TYNWALD HILL,* an ancient artificial mount about
twelve feet in height, eighty yards in circumference,
seven feet in diameter at the top, and encircled by
three receding terraces or rows of seats, cut in its
sides, and surmounting each other at regular distances from the base; while, at the eastern point, a
small flight of steps conducts to the summit. This

---

* From this hill, "about a thousand years ago, the Norwegians governed the Sudreyjar. Although the British Parliament makes laws for England, Ireland, and Scotland, they
are of no validity in the Isle of Man, unless they are in
accordance with the ancient laws and liberties of the island,
and, after being confirmed by its own Parliament, are proclaimed from Tynwald Hill. The Manx Parliament, whose
origin is lost in the mists of remote antiquity, but whose
establishment is usually ascribed to the Danish king Orry
(Erik ?), who settled in the island in the beginning of the tenth
century, consists of the three estates of the island: 1st, the
king or superior lord; 2nd, the governor and council; 3rd,
the twenty-four representatives of the island (Keys or Taxiaxi)
... Amongst all the Scandinavian Thing-hills or Thing-walls
(Thingavellir) that can be traced in the old Danish part of
England, in the Norwegian part of Scotland, as well as in the
Orkneys and Shetland Islands, and which also formerly
existed in Iceland, Norway, and throughout the North, Tynwald in Man is the only one now in use."—Worsaae.

"The ancient Scandinavian courts were held in the open air,
generally on natural hills or artificial tumuli. Their colonies
in England and Scotland adopted the same practice, and hence
many eminences, erroneously supposed to be Roman camps,
still retain the name of Ting or Ding—such as Dingwall, the
Tinwald Hill in Dumfriesshire, the Tynwald Hill in the Isle
of Man, Tingvalla in Iceland, &c."—Palgrave.

circular mound—a remarkable memorial of the early power of the Northmen in Man—is covered all over with a beautiful greensward : it stands on St. John's Green, about two miles and a half from Peel. "The place is situated in the calm green bosom of a lovely vale, walled in on all sides at irregular distances by lofty hills, and the view from the mount, around the circumference of its boundary, has an air of security, beauty, and seclusion, that is extremely pleasing." The word Tynwald (originally Thingvöllr), is derived from *Thing*, signifying in the ancient language of the north, the place of convention, a court of justice or assizes, or a popular assembly ; and *völlr*, a field, a green, a vale. The word is thus defined by Haldorson :—"Thingvöllr=campus v. locus comitiorum." For the protection of public liberty, the Scandinavian Thing (pronounced Ting) at which generally all the freemen of the nation had a right to attend, was held in the open air. The Tynwald Court of Man, which can be convoked at the will of the Lieutenant-Governor, possesses both the judicial and the legislative power. What the three estates agree on becomes a law ; but it is not in force until it has been promulgated from Tynwald Hill. Formerly it was the

practice to read the new acts at full length in the English and Manx languages; but now the reading in English and Manx of the titles and marginal notes only of all new acts is held to be legal publication thereof. The ceremony of proclaiming the laws takes place on every successive 5th of July. The people come from all parts of the island, and assemble round the mount in thousands. The Lieutenant-Governor and all the high dignitaries of the isle attend divine service in the adjacent church. They then walk in procession to the mount, on which a canopy and chair are placed for the Lieutenant-Governor. The chief officials, the Keys, and the clergy occupy the three rows of seats cut in the sides of the hill. The first court of which any record has been preserved was held here in 1417 by Sir John Stanley. Being unacquainted with the ceremonies observed by former kings, he sent queries to the Deemsters and Keys, to which he required written answers. The following curious account of the forms and ceremonies which had been observed at Tynwald Hill prior to the accession of the Stanleys to the throne, was furnished, and may be seen at page 5 of the Statute Book :—

"Our Doughtfull and Gratious Lord, this is the Constitution of old Time, the which we have given in our Days, how yee should be governed on your Tinwald Day. First, you shall come thither in your Royall Array, as a King ought to do, by the Prerogatives and Royalties of the Land of Mann. And upon the Hill of Tinwald sitt in a Chaire, covered with Royall \'loath and Cushions, and your Visage into the East, and your s vord before you, holden with the point upward ; your Barrons in the third degree sitting beside you, and your beneficed Men and your Deemsters before you sitting; and your Clearke, your Knights, Esquires and Yeomen, about you in the third Degree ; and the worthiest Men in your Land to be called in before your Deemsters, if you will ask any Thing of them, and to hear the Government of your Land and your Will; and the Commons to stand without the Circle of the Hill, with three Clearkes in their Surplisses. And your Deemsters shall make

Call in the Coroner of Glanfaba; and he shall call in all the Coroners of Mann, and their Yards in their Hands, with their weapons upon them, either Sword or Axe. And the Moares, that is, to Witt of every Sheading. Then the Chief Coroner, that is, the Coroner of Glanfaba, shall make Affence, upon Paine of Life and Lyme, that noe Man make any Disturbance or Stirr in the Time of Tinwald, or any Murmur or Rising in the King's Presence, upon Paine of Hanging and Drawing. And then shall let your Barrons and all other know you to be their King and Lord, and what Time you were here you received the land as Heyre Apparent in your Father's Days."

These preliminary forms are still observed; and then the titles of the laws which have been enacted during the past year are read to the assembled people.

A little to the north of the hill, in Follagh-y-Vannin-road, an ancient tumulus may be seen. At a short distance to the east stands the church of St. John the Baptist—an elegant edifice built of granite : a vague tradition prevails that a temple dedicated to Thor once stood on its site. At the base of the steeple is a mutilated cross with the following Runic inscription :—

"INA SVRTR RAIST RUNAR THSER,"

i.e., "Ina (Henna?) the Swarthy engraved these runes." It may not be superfluous to remark that *raist* or *reist* is the preterite of *rista* to carve or engrave : it must not be confounded with *raisti* or *reisti*, the preterite of *reisa* to raise up or erect (see Rask's Grammar, pp. 126 and 167). *Thser* is obviously an abbreviation of *thesser :* that reading was first given by the present writer. See inscription No. 5, Chapter VI.

Some years ago, a slab, engraven with characters which no one can decipher, was dug up in this parish.

About half a mile to the east of Tynwald Hill is—

BALLACRAINE. Pursuing the northern road from this place, we enter a wild and romantic ravine called Glen Mooar, and afterwards Glen Helen, arriving in.

a short time at Rhennass Suspension-bridge and
Swiss Cottage; about a mile and a half from which,
further up this lovely glen (named after the second
daughter of the late Mr. Marsden), is the charming
waterfall of Rhennass. To reach this, we must
deviate from the high road. A narrow footpath by
the side of the stream that meanders through the
glen, conducts the visitor to the cascade, which is
formed by a mountain torrent rushing impetuously
over a precipice of considerable height, called in days
of yore Rinn-eas, *i.e.*, Waterfall point or height
(Irish and Gaelic *rinn*, a point or top; and *eas* a
waterfall). The surrounding scenery is remarkably
fine. Whoever of the thousands that annually seek
health and recreation amid the varied beauties of the
isle has failed to visit this delightful spot, has unquestionably omitted from his tour one of the most
picturesque localities it possesses.

The road now ascends the steep and rocky Craig-
Willis Hill. Having gained the summit, we come to
Cronk-y-Voddey, (*i.e.*, hill of the dog), on which is a
neat chapel-of-ease, dedicated to St. John the Evan-
gelist. In this neigbourhood are many objects
deserving of notice. Manannan's Chair and several
ancient forts on the estate of Corvalley, will repay a
visit. Continuing our journey we reach the parish
of—

MICHAEL : the scenery on the route is full of interest and beauty. Sartfell, Slieau-ny-Fraughane,
Slieau Hearn, and other mountains,

"Rearing their crests amid the cloudless skies,"

will be perceived on the eastern side of the parish.
Passing Cronk Urleigh (anciently called Reneurling*),
on which District Courts, and occasionally Tynwald

---

* Reneurling is obviously a corruption of Rinn-urley, *i.e.*,
eagle hill.

Courts were held down to the year 1428, we soon arrive at the village of Michael, at the entrance of which are the Court-house and the Mitre-hotel. Near its centre stands the parish church, an elegant and spacious edifice, erected in 1835.

In the churchyard is the tomb of the celebrated Bishop Wilson, a prelate whose memory will ever be revered in the Isle of Man. The inscription states that—"Sleeping in Jesus, here lieth the body of Thomas Wilson, D.D., Lord Bishop of this Isle, who died March 5th, 1755, aged 93, and in the 58th year of his consecration. This monument was erected by his son, Thomas Wilson, D.D., a native of this parish, who, in obedience to the express commands of his father, declines giving him the character he justly deserved. Let this Island speak the rest." The graves of Bishop Hildesley and Crigan may also be seen. On the walls of the churchyard there are several ancient monumental crosses with Runic inscriptions. Translations of these inscriptions are given in Worsaae's "Danes and Northmen," and in Prof. Munch's works. The cross on the south side of the gate is

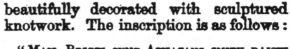

beautifully decorated with sculptured knotwork. The inscription is as follows :

"MAIL BRIGTI SUNR ATHACANS SMITH RAISTI KRUS THANA FUR SALU SINA SIN BRUKUIN GAUT GIRTHI THANA AUK ALA I MAUN,"

i.e., "Malbrigd, son of Athacan [the] smith, erected this cross for his soul . . . Gaut made this [cross] and all [the crosses] on Man." See inscription No. 11, Chap. VI.

That which stands on the north side of the gate is much defaced: various sculptured figures, including a harper, a stag, a dog, &c., may be seen on it. The inscription, which contains several Keltic names, is as follows :—

"MAL LUMKUN RAISTI KRUS THANA EFTIR MAL MURU FUSTRA SINA DATIR DUFGALS KANA ES ATHISI ATI,"

i.e., "Mal Lumkun erected this cross to Malmora, his foster-mother, daughter of Dugald the Keen (or Clever), whom Athisi had to wife." See inscription No. 8, Chapter VI.

Opposite to the churchyard gate stands another cross, profusely ornamented with a variety of sculptured figures and animals, representing a stag-hunt. One of the edges is decorated with interlaced work ; on the other is the inscription :—

"JUALFIR SUNR THURULFS EINS RAUTHA RISTI KRUS THANA AFT FRITHU MUTHUR SINA,"

i.e., "Joalf, son of Thorolf the Red, erected this cross to his mother Frida." See inscription No. 7, Chapter VI. This cross was found many years ago, about a foot below the surface of the ground, in what is called the chapel-field, on the vicar's glebe. Fragments of crosses on the churchyard wall have the following inscriptions:—

"GRIM RISTI KRUS THAN EFT RUMUN,"

i.e., "Grim erected this cross to Hromund;" and—

"KRUS THAN AFTIR,"

i.e., "(A. B. erected) this cross to (C. D.)." See inscriptions Nos. 9 and 4, Chapter VI. In the church is the fragment of another richly sculptured cross, bearing the name of Grim the Swarthy— "Grims eins Suarta." See inscription No. 10, Chapter VI. Near the chancel of the old church is another cross, much mutilated.

BISHOP'S COURT, a domain of about three hundred acres, the mansion of which is the episcopal palace of the diocese, is a mile from the village. Part of the edifice is of high antiquity: it was anciently called Torkilstadt. The venerable trees in the midst of which it stands were planted by Bishop Wilson. The memorial chapel recently erected by the present diocesan is deserving of notice. In the vicinity of the episcopal palace is the Bishop's Glen, a charming spot, rich with the most beautiful vegetation: here the lover of the picturesque will find ample gratification.

Every tourist with leisure at command should pay a visit to Glen Trunk, Glen Balleira, Glen Wyllyn, and Glen Mooar, all of which are famed for the romantic beauty of their scenery. Glen Wyllyn, which is noted for the purity and health-bestowing qualities of its air, has been appropriately styled the insular Montpellier.

The stream which flows through the singularly picturesque glen at Ballaskir, in pouring over a precipice upwards of sixty feet in height, forms a splendid cascade called Spooyt Vane, *i.e.*, the white spout. A rude wooden bridge spans the river a few yards above the waterfall, contiguous to which, perched on an eminence, is an ancient Treen chapel.

CHAPTER XI.

EXCURSIONS, ITINERARIES, ETC.

> " It is a goodly sight to see
> What heaven hath done for this delicious land!
> What fruits of fragrance blush on every tree!
> What goodly prospects o'er the hills expand!
>
> BYRON.

To THOSE who desire to explore the beauties of Ellan Vannin veg veen ("Little dear or favourite Isle of Man"), a few hints with respect to the excursions they should make will not prove unacceptable. The following places are especially worthy of a visit :—

First Excursion.—PORT SODERICK and GREENWICK: two beautiful rocky inlets, easily accessible, the former about four miles, the latter about six miles and a half, from Douglas.

Second Excursion.—RUSHEN ABBEY, PORT ERIN, and the CHASMS: the ruins of the Abbey are charmingly situated on the banks of a rivulet in the vicinity of Ballasalla: Port Erin is a most romantic spot, and possesses great attractions in the way of wild rocky scenery: the prospects from the majestic cliffs contiguous to the Chasms are inexpressibly grand.

Third Excursion.—CASTLETOWN, STACK OF SCARLET, FLESHWICK, and COLBY: the old Castle will well repay a visit: Scarlet Stack is said to owe its formation to the operation of an ancient submarine volcano:

Fleshwick is a romantic cove situate at the southern extremity of the mountain called Ennyn Mooar: Colby glen is a charming place, much resorted to by tourists.

Fourth Excursion.—PEEL and GLEN MEAY WATER-FALL: the ruins of the Castle and Cathedral are the objects most worthy of attention in Peel: Glen Meay is a green sequestered vale of the rarest and most varied beauty; visitors repair thither from year to year without weariness or satiety.

Fifth Excursion.—DALBY *viâ* FOXDALE (crossing the acclivity of SOUTH BARRULL): there is a constant succession of sublime and romantic scenery in travelling from Foxdale to Dalby.

Sixth Excursion.—INGEBRECK, and thence by mountain road to MICHAEL and SPOOYT VANE (Waterfall): the prospect from the high lands a little beyond Ingebreck is very extensive and beautiful; some of the finest views in the island are obtainable here: the waterfall called Spooyt Vane is well worthy of particular notice.

Seventh Excursion.—RHENNASS: fairer spot than GLEN HELEN cannot be found in the Isle of Man; in point of natural beauty it may perhaps be placed first among the dales of Mona. The view from the precipice near the waterfall will afford unqualified pleasure to every admirer of picturesque scenery.

Eighth Excursion.—RAMSEY *viâ* BALLACRAINE: the whole of the drive to Ramsey is a succession of the most splendid views: the Bishop's Glen (in Michael), a delightful place, shadowy with graceful trees, will amply repay a visit.

Ninth Excursion.—SNAEFELL *viâ* KEPPEL-GATE: the tourist should, if possible, ascend Snaefell. The most eligible route to take is to go from Douglas direct to Keppel-gate, from which point a fine road extends northward, winding round the sides of the mountains and crossing the eastern acclivity of

Snaefell: hence a ten minutes' walk brings the visitor to the summit, which commands a magnificent prospect. Should the tourist have time, we would recommend him to descend the western declivity of the mountain and explore Sulby Glen, the scenery of which is extremely wild and grand.

Tenth Excursion.—LAXEY and GLEN ROY: Laxey lies in a valley of beauty and verdure, surrounded by lofty hills. The chief objects of interest here are the Mines and the Great Waterwheel: the excursion to Glen Roy should on no account be omitted.

Eleventh Excursion. — BALLAGLASS WATERFALL: this beautiful waterfall, a constant object of attraction to multitudes of visitors, is situate in the midst of lovely rural scenery.

In order to facilitate the perambulations of tourists who may refer to these pages, we subjoin several itineraries.

DOUGLAS TO CASTLETOWN (New Road).

Miles from
Douglas.

¼..Ruins of an ancient bridge. See Legend in Chap. XIII.

½..The Nunnery, where King Robert Bruce spent a night in 1313.

1 ..Site of ancient chapel dedicated to St. Bridget.

1¼..Junction with the old road.

1½..Kewague.

2 ..Middle Hill. The road on the right leads to Kirk Braddan.

3 ..Richmond Hill.

3½..Ancient cemetery in the lane on the right.

4 ..Mount Murray mansion, which formerly belonged to Lord Henry Murray. Two roads branching to the right conduct to Glen Darragh, &c.

4¼..Road on the right leading to Old Fort, on the estate called Ferk.

5 ..Road on the left conducting to Greenwick, &c.

6 ..Ballalona-bridge, said to be the scene of his Satanic Majesty's frequent exploits.

8 ..Ballsalla village: Rushen Abbey: Ancient Bridge: road to Cas-na-awin, Derby Haven, Langness, &c.

Miles from
Douglas.

9 ..King William's College: Hango Hill.
10 ..Castletown.

DOUGLAS TO CASTLETOWN (Old Road).

1¼..Junction of old and new roads.
1¾..Ellenbrook.
2¼..Oak Hill: New Church: Path on the left leading to Port
    Soderick.
3 ..Hampton Court.
3½..Road leading to Port Soderick.
4 ..Croga Bridge.
5¾..Stone-circle on estate called Ballakelly.
6¼..Path conducting to Greenwick: Cronk-ny-Marroo, &c.
7 ..Santon Church.
8 ..Ballasalla.
10 ..Castletown.

DOUGLAS TO RAMSEY (*viâ* Laxey).

⅛..Villa Marina Hotel: Marine Promenade.
1 ..Castle Mona Hotel, formerly the residence of the Duke of
    Athole: Falcon Cliff.
1½..Strathallan Crescent and Park: Derby Castle.
2 ..Onchan village: St. Catherine's (Runic crosses): Nursery
    Gardens: Onchan Church (Runic crosses): Road on
    the right leading to Growdale: Road on the left con-
    ducting to Glen Doo, Cronk-ny-Mona, Keppel-gate, &c.
3¼..White Bridge and White Bridge Hill.
5 ..Road on the right leading to old church of Lonan (Runic
    crosses): and to Growdale.
5¾..Cloven Stones: Path leading to Garwick.
7 ..New Church of Lonan.
8 ..Laxey Village: Mines: Great Water-wheel: Lord
    Henry's Well: The so-called grave of King "Orry!":
    Stone-circle: Road leading to Glen Roy: Road con-
    ducting to Snaefell (height 2024 feet).
11½..Road on the right leading to Ballaglass Waterfall, Cornah,
    and Maughold Church.
15 ..Ballure Glen: Ballure Bridge: Albert Tower.
16 ..Ramsey.

DOUGLAS TO RAMSEY (*viâ* Ballacraine).

1 ..Ballabrooie.

Miles from
Douglas.

1¼..Quarter Bridge: Port-e-Chee.
1¾..Kirby: Braddan Church: Ancient Fortification.
2¼..Union Mills: Dalrymple Memorial Chapel.
4¼..Crosby.
5¼..Ruins of St. Trinion's Church.
5¾..Greeba Mountain: Greeba Tower and Castle.
7¾..Ballacraine.
8 ..Ballig Bridge: Cronk-y-Killey.
     Glen Mooar and Glen Helen.
9¼..Rhennass Suspension Bridge: Path to Waterfall.
10¼..Summit of Craig Willis Hill.
11 ..Cronk-y-Voddey (i.e., Hill of the Dog): Church of St. John
     the Evangelist: Road on the left leading to the old
     fort on estate called Corvalley, to Manannan's Chair,
     and Spooyt Vane (waterfall).
11¼..Glen Cannell.
12¼..Ballaskir Glen.
13 ..Bergarrow: Road on the left conducting to Spooyt Vane
     (waterfall), Cronk Giucklee, Cronk-y-Berry, and Glen
     Mooar.
13½..Cronk Urleigh (i.e., Eagle Hill); District Courts and
     occasionally Tynwald Courts were held here down to
     the year 1428.
14¼..Michael Village and Church (Runic crosses and Bishop
     Wilson's tomb): Roads conducting respectively to
     Glen Wyllyn, Glen Balleira, and Glen Trunk.
15 ..Michael Vicarage, nearly opposite to which is an ancient
     barrow.
15¼..Cronk-y-Crodda, where many sepulchral urns have been
     found.
15½..Mitre Cottage.
16 ..Bishop's Court, the residence of the Bishop of Sodor and
     Man: The Bishop's Glen: Road on the left leading
     to Orrisdale, Keil Pharlane, &c.
17½..Ballaugh Village and Church (Runic cross at the old
     church): Road on the right conducting to Druidale
     and Ravensdale (mountain road thence to Injebreck).
19½..Sulby, with its romantic glen (Snaefell may be ascended
     from this glen: Cronk Samark: Road on the left
     leading to Jurby, Andreas, &c.
22 ..Lezayre Church.
23 ..Sky Hill, a famous hill in Manx history: Milntown:
     Road on the right conducting to Snaefell.
24 ..Ramsey.

DOUGLAS TO PEEL.

Miles from
Douglas.

½..Cowin's Strawberry Gardens.

1 ..Ballabrooie (*i.e.*, the place of river banks), where a spa was discovered many years ago.

1¼..Quarter Bridge: Port-e-Chee mansion stands on the right; it was one of the first residences of the late Duke of Athole in this isle.

1¾..Kirby, the residence of his Honour Deemster Drinkwater, and formerly the property of Colonel Wilks, Governor of St. Helena, is on the south side of the road: Braddan Church (Runic crosses): Road leading to the Cemetery, to the Strang, to Baldwin, and to Injebreck.

2¾..The Union Mills: Dalrymple Memorial Chapel: Road on the left conducting to Mount Murray, Glen Darragh, &c.

4 ..Road on the left leading to Glen Darragh, to Treen Chapels, to Stone-circle, to old forts at Balla Nicholas, to St. Mark's, &c. Slieau Chiarn (*i.e.*, the Mountain of the Lord) may be seen: Marown New Church: Aiken's Castle.

4½..Crosby Village: The south road leads to Marown Old Church, to the so-called Chair of St. Patrick, &c. The north road conducts (across the mountains) to Little London, Rhennass (waterfall), &c.

5¼..Ruins of St. Trinion's Church: The Round Meadow. See Chapter XIII. for an account of the Buggane of the church and the Phynnodderee of the meadow.

5¾..Greeba Mountain : Greeba Tower and Castle.

6 ..Northop.

7¼..Ballacraine: Junction of roads conducting respectively to Castletown, Douglas, Peel, and Ramsey.

8 ..Tynwald Hill: Tumulus (in Follagh-y-Vannin-road): Church of St. John the Baptist (Runic cross): Slieau Whuaillan (*i.e.*, Mountain of the Whelp).

9¼..Peel Cemetery.

10 ..Wesleyan School.

10½..Peel. It is contemplated to construct a railway between Douglas and Peel.

PEEL TO MICHAEL.

Miles from
Peel.

1¾..Road on the left conducting to the shore.

2¾..Knocksharry: The hill called the Giant's Fingers is not far distant.

Miles from
Peel.

3 .. Glen Brough.

3¾..A circular mound may be seen on an eminence to the right; under it is a kist-vaen.

4 Glen Cam (*i.e.*, Crooked Glen). It forms the ecclesiastical boundary between German and Michael.

5½..Glen Mooar: on a neighbouring rocky height is the burial-place of some distinguished viking; a rude stone, about six feet high and five feet broad, marks his resting-place: Road on the right leading to Spooyt Vane (waterfall).

6½..Glen Wyllyn, the insular Montpellier.

7 ..Michael Court House, village, and church.

CASTLETOWN TO PEEL.

Miles from
Castletown.

1¼..Malew Church: Road leading to Port Erin, Arbory, Colby, and Fleshwick.

2¼..Ruins of Rushen Abbey: Ancient bridge called the Crossag.

4¼..Road conducting to St. Mark's.

5 ..In this neighbourhood formerly stood the "Black Fort" mentioned by Sir Walter Scott in "Peveril of the Peak:" South Barrull (height 1584 feet): Road leading to the Round Table.

6¼..Foxdale Mines.

7¼.. Waterfall at Hamilton Bridge.

9 ..Ballacraine.

9½..St. John's Church and Tynwald Hill.

11 ..Cemetery.

12 ..Peel.

CASTLETOWN TO PORT ST. MARY (Shore Route).

1 ..Balladoole House, approached by a pretty avenue of trees.

1¼..Road on the right leading to Round Table, &c.: Road on the left leading to Poolvash Marble Quarries.

2 ..Submerged Forest on sea-shore to the left.

2½..Road on the right conducting to Colby, &c.: Kentraugh, the residence of E. M. Gawne, Esq., Speaker of the House of Keys.

3½..Mount Gawne Hotel: road on the right leading to Port Erin.

4 Giant's Quoiting Stones: Road conducting to Craigneesh and the Chasms.

4½..Port St. Mary.

CASTLETOWN TO PORT ST. MARY (Inland Route).

Miles from
Castletown.

1¼..Road on the left leading to Port St. Mary, &c.
2 ..Road on the right conducting to Ballasalla, &c.
2¼..Friary of Brymaken, founded, according to Tanner, A.D.
     1373.
2½..Arbory Church.
3 ..Colby Village.
3¾..Road on the right leading to Ballacorkish Mines, &c.
4¼..In a meadow on the right, Ragnvald IV., King of Man,
     was murdered, A.D. 1248 : Rushen Church : road on
     the right leading to Fairy Hill.
4¾..Four Roads—that on the right conducting to Port Erin,
     that on the left to Castletown.
5½..Port St. Mary.

For the information of visitors, a list of charges
for vehicles is subjoined :—

*For a carriage and pair of horses, to carry not more than ten
persons besides the driver, and to be detained for the day, if the
hirer desires it.*

To Ramsey	. . . .	.and back	20/-,	driver	3/-
" Kirk Michael	. . .	"	20/-	"	3/-
" Ramsey, *via* Kirk Michael	. .	"	25/-	"	3/-
" Peel, Port Erin, and Port St. Mary	"	25/-	"	3/-	
" Glen Meay	. . . .	"	18/-	"	2/6
" Port Erin and Port St. Mary	. .	"	20/-	"	3/-
" Castletown	. . . .	"	15/-	"	2/-
" Peel	. . . .	"	15/-	"	2/-
" Laxey	. . . .	"	15/-	"	2/-

For one mile, and back again, 3/-; for every additional mile,
or part of a mile, and back again, 1/4.

BY TIME.—For the first hour, or fraction of an hour, 3/-; for
every additional half hour, or fraction of a half hour, after the
first hour 1/6.

For Sociable, or Long Car, for the day.

	For each person which it is licensed to carry.
To Ramsey, *via* Kirk Michael . . .	3/6
" Ramsey, *via* Laxey	3/-
" Peel and Castletown	3/-
" Peel, Port Erin, and Port St. Mary . .	3/-
" Castletown	2/-
" Peel	2/-
" Laxey	2/-

For a car or carriage, drawn by one horse, to carry not more than four persons, besides the driver, and may be detained for the day, if the hirer desires it.

To Ramsey . . . . and back 12/-, driver 2/-
" Ramsey, *via* Kirk Michael . . " 15/- do.
" Kirk Michael . . . . " 12/- do.
" Castletown . . . . . " 8/- do.
" Peel . . . . . . " 8/- do.
" Laxey . . . . . " 8/- do.
" Peel and Glen Meay . . . " 10/- do.
" Peel, Port Erin, and Port St. Mary " 15/- do.

For one mile, and back again, 1/6 ; for every additional mile, or part of a mile, and back again, 9d.

BY TIME.—For the first hour, or fraction of an hour, 1/6 ; for every additional half hour, or fraction of a half hour, after the first hour, 9d.

———

CHAPTER XII.

VOYAGE ROUND THE ISLAND.

"But it is not the beautiful only lives
In this happy land, but the wild sublime,
Torrent and chasm and mountain hoar
Are there from the oldest olden time."
DR. KENEALEY.

DURING the summer months, the steamers of the Packet Company frequently perform the voyage round the isle. The coast scenery of Mona, the

"Isle which stands
As Neptune's park, ribbed and paled in
With rocks unscaleable,"

is singularly wild and picturesque. After leaving Douglas Harbour, the

TOWER OF REFUGE, on Conister* Rock attracts our attention. See Wordsworth's sonnet, in Chapter VII. The first object of interest which presents itself in crossing Douglas Bay is

CASTLE MONA, which was built by the late Duke of Athole. A description of this noble edifice will be found in Chapter VII.

DERBY CASTLE will also be seen. Beyond it are several secluded creeks, much resorted to by bathers.

ONCHAN HARBOUR next appears. Many caverns may be seen in the neighbouring cliffs.

BANKS's HOWE, *i.e.*, headland, forms the northern extremity of Douglas Bay. After passing it, we arrive at

GROWDALE. The ancient church of Lonan is not far distant.

CLAY HEAD, formerly called *Laxi Poynt*, is next rounded; and we pass

GARWICK, into which flows a pretty rivulet.

LAXEY BAY; at the north of which, Laxey village, a place greatly resorted to by visitors, stands. The mines, the monster water-wheel, the beautiful glen, Lord Henry's Well, and the so-called tomb of King Orry, form the grand attractions of this little village. In fine weather, the lofty summits of Snaefell and Bein-y-Phot (the former 2024, the latter 1772 feet above the level of the sea) are distinctly visible. Tourists frequently ascend Snaefell from Laxey.

---

* The name Conister is perhaps a corruption of the Irish words Cuan aistre (pronounced Con-naister), signifying "the harbour or bay of the expedition, or journey." This may have been the ancient appellation of Douglas Bay. Compare Connemara (Cuan-an-ir-more), *i.e.*, "the bay of the great waters." In days of yore, the Keltic inhabitants of Man evidently kept up a connection with Ireland and Scotland. The three countries were collectively denominated Trefod, *i.e.*, "three lands." The word is thus defined in Cormac's Glossary: "Trefod *i.e.*, tri foide, *i.e.*, Erind, Manaind, acas Albain." The writer of this glossary was killed at the battle of Bealach Mughna, A.D. 908.

LAXEY HEAD is next passed. Continuing our
voyage along the shore, which now exhibits a succession of bold, abrupt, and rugged cliffs, we soon reach
CORNAH HAVEN, into which flows the Dhoon river.
The waterfall of Ballaglass, not far distant, is well
worthy of a visit. Shortly afterwards we approach
PORT MOOAR; and then
MAUGHOLD HEAD, the most eastern point of the
Isle of Man, 373 feet in height, named after the
celebrated saint of the sixth century. A view of the
church, which is dedicated to him, may be obtained.
Saint Maughold's Well may also be seen on this bold
promontory. On the first Sunday in August, the
natives, according to ancient custom, make a pilgrim-
age to drink its waters, which are noted for their
medicinal qualities. After rounding this lofty headland, we enter
RAMSEY BAY, on the margin of which the town of
Ramsey stands. About seven centuries ago, a battle
was fought in this bay between the fleets of Gudröd,
King of Man, and Somerled the Surly, Thane of
Argyle. In 1313, King Robert Bruce landed here,
and shortly afterwards laid siege to Castle Rushen.
The town, it will be seen, is backed by successive
ranges of high lands, culminating in the noble
mountain of North Barrull, which is 1842 feet in
height. Barrull signifies the "big peak." Albert
Tower, erected to commemorate the visit of her
Majesty the Queen and the late Prince Consort in
1847, is a very conspicuous object.
THE POINT OF AYRE and the Lighthouse next
demand attention. This is the northernmost point
of the Isle of Man. It will amuse visitors to be told
that Ragnvald I., a magician, and King of Man in
the tenth century, attempted to build a bridge from
this place to Burrough Head, in Galloway, which
is sixteen miles distant. After rounding the point,
we soon pass

BLUE HEAD, not far from which is

THE LHANE or LAANE. Here, according to tradition, "Orry," the celebrated King of Man, landed, and was met on the beach by a deputation of the inhabitants.

CRONK-NARRAI-SHAGE, *i.e.*, the hill of the watch by day, is near LLEN MOOAR.

JURBY POINT, on which is CRONK MOOAR, is next passed. The ancient name of Jurby was probably Ivarsby, *i.e.*, Ivar's village. In 1098, a famous battle was fought in Jurby parish, in which the women of the north of the island took part. For particulars, see the chapter on the civil history of the isle. We next approach

ORRISDALE HEAD and GLEN TRUNK, and obtain a view of the tower of Bishop's Court (the residence of the Bishop of Sodor and Man), and shortly afterwards of the village of

MICHAEL, with the mountains Slieau Hearn, Viael, Slieau-ny-Fraughane, and Sartfell in the background. Passing

GLEN BALLEIRA, which is famed for its beauty,

GLEN WYLLYN next demands attention. It is called the insular Montpellier, and is much resorted to by tourists. Continuing our voyage we approach

GLEN MOOAR. The beautiful waterfall called Spooyt Vane is not far distant from this glen. About two miles to the south of Glen Mooar some remarkable caves may be seen on the coast.

ORRY'S HEAD is next approached; and proceeding still southward we reach

PEEL CASTLE. The ruins of the cathedral, of the so-called church of St. Patrick, of the palace of the Bishops, of the palace of the Stanleys, an ancient round Tower, and a Runic cross with inscription, are the principal objects of interest within its walls. In 1397, Thomas, Earl of Warwick, was imprisoned here. In 1440, Eleanor, Duchess of Gloucester, was banished to the the Isle of Man and was confined in this castle. A legend, connected with Peel Castle, concerning the Moddey Doo, or Black dog, will be found in Chapter XIII. The summit of

CORRIN'S FOLLY, a tower built about fifty years ago by a person named Corrin, as a mausoleum for his family, may be perceived.

CONTRARY HEAD is the first headland south of Peel. This name was bestowed upon it from the fact that opposite flood streams meet here. Proceeding about three miles to the south we pass

GLEN MEAY, through which a rivulet flows into the sea. At a short distance up this sequestered glen there is a beautiful waterfall, a description of which will be found in chapter X. Passing southward we approach

DALBY POINT. From this point to Brada, and from Port Erin to Spanish Head, the stupendous cliffs plunge almost sheer down into the deep blue water. No words can convey any adequate idea of the sublime scenery of this rock-bound coast. We here behold the rugged Cronk-na-Irey-Lhaa, or Hill of the Rising Day, which descends precipitously into the sea; its altitude is 1445 feet. The so-called cemetery of the ancient Kings of Man, and a famous well (connected with which there are several legends), may be seen on this mountain. Proceeding still southward, we come to

FLESHWICK, the scenery of which is exceedingly wild and picturesque. At the south of this romantic bay stands

BRADA HEAD, where there are mines, producing copper and lead. After passing it we reach

PORT ERIN. A description of this charming place is given in Chapter VIII. After

THE MULL HILLS, the south-western extremity of the island are passed, we come to

KITTERLAND, a rocky islet between the mainland

and the Calf of Man. In 1852 a terrific explosion of gunpowder took place on board the brig *Lily* (which was stranded on this islet), by which thirty-two seamen lost their lives.

THE CALF, which is well worthy of a visit, next attracts our attention. There is a double lighthouse upon it. A ruin upon the highest part, called Bushell's House, was formerly the residence of a recluse, a friend of the celebrated Lord Bacon. Several insulated rocks may be seen (the stacks on the western side, and the Eye and Sugar-loaf rocks on the south-eastern). A beacon has been erected on the Thousla or Tuesdale Rock, in the Sound. The Calf is the resort of innumerable sea-birds ; here may be heard

"The myriad shriek of wheeling ocean-fowl."

We next approach

SPANISH HEAD, (so called, it is said, because some relics of the famous armada were thrown on this coast in 1588). In this bold headland may be seen the twelve chasms which are so much resorted to by visitors. Perched in a recess on its summit is a stone circle, probably indicating the burial-place of some Scandinavian chieftain. In a short time we pass

PERWICK BAY, and reach

PORT ST. MARY, a thriving fishing village, and

POOLVASH, celebrated for its black marble quarries. The stone forming the steps of St. Paul's Cathedral, London, was obtained from this place. We now approach

SCARLET POINT, and the STACK of Scarlet; and, continuing our voyage, we pass

CASTLETOWN BAY, and obtain a view of the town, of Rushen Castle, and of King William's College. Proceeding, we come to the peninsula of

LANGNESS, *i.e.*, Long Naze. At its extremity are dangerous rocks called the Skerranes. After passing

DRESWICK POINT, we soon arrive at

ST. MICHAEL'S ISLET, which stands at the northern extremity of Langness. A small ruined church, and Derby Fort, may be seen on it. At the west of this islet is

DERBY HAVEN. Proceeding, we obtain a distant view of

GREENWICK, near which are two ancient fortifications; and after passing the bold and lofty promontory called

ST. ANNE'S HEAD, we approach.

PORT SODERICK, a noted place for pic-nic parties during the summer months. In the rocks on the south side there is a curious cavern. Beyond this little bay the coast presents a succession of bold and rugged cliffs, extending to

DOUGLAS HEAD, on which the lighthouse stands. In a few minutes we pass

FORT ANNE, and enter Douglas Harbour, thus completing the circumnavigation of the Isle of Man.

CHAPTER XIII.

LEGENDS OF THE ISLE OF MAN.

"Many a tale
Traditionary round the mountains hung;
And many a legend, peopling the dark woods,
Nourished imagination."

SIR WALTER SCOTT, in his "Letters on Demonolgy and Witchcraft," remarks :—"We find from the ingenious researches of Mr. Waldron, that the Isle of Man, beyond other places in Britain, was a peculiar depository of the fairy traditions, which, on the island being conquered by the Norse, became in all

probability chequered with those of Scandinavia,
from a source peculiar and more direct than that by
which they reached Scotland or Ireland." Most of
the following legends are extracted from the work
alluded to by the distinguished novelist; a few are
taken from Train's History and Wood's Account of
of the Isle of Man.

THE TREASURES OF THE SEA.

"I saw

Wedges of gold, great anchors, heaps of pearl,
Inestimable stones, unvalued jewels,
All scatter'd in the bottom of the sea."

SHAKESPEARE.

A project was set on foot some time ago for
searching for treasures in the sea. Several vessels
were got ready without delay, and many machines
were made to enable the divers to descend into the
sea. One of these machines was made of glass, cased
with tough leather. The vessel on board which it
was placed happened to sail near to the Isle of Man,
and the captain having heard that several large ships
containing immense treasures had been wrecked upon
the coasts, determined to let down the machine, and
in it the adventurous diver who was to search for
treasures at the bottom of the ocean. This was
accordingly done, the diver descending to a great
depth. As he continued from time to time to pull
the rope (which was the sign for those in the vessel
to increase the quantity), they obtained more rope,
and lowered him to a still greater depth. At last
they found themselves entirely out of rope. A mathe-
matician, who was on board, assured the captain that
the diver must have descended from the surface of

the water more than twice the number of leagues
that the moon is computed to be distant from the
earth! Having, therefore, no more rope, they were
compelled to turn the wheel, which by degrees
brought the diver up again. He seemed very much
annoyed at being pulled up, and declared that if he
could have gone a little farther, his labours would
have been crowned with complete success. Every-
body was of course extremely anxious to hear what
discoveries had been made, but he declined to utter a
word until he had recruited himself with a hearty
swill of brandy. Having obtained this, he related
the following story:—"After I had passed the region
of the fishes, I descended into a purer element, clear
as the air in the serenest and most unclouded day,
through which, as I passed, I saw distinctly the
bottom of the watery world, paved with coral and
beautiful pebbles, which glittered like the sunbeams
reflected on a glass. As you may imagine, I longed
to tread the delightful paths, and never felt more
exquisite delight than when the machine in which I
was enclosed grazed upon the bottom. Looking
through the windows of the machine, I saw large
streets and noble squares on every side, ornamented
with pyramids of crystal not inferior in brilliancy to
the finest diamonds, and beautiful edifices built of
pearl, embossed in various figures with shells of all
colours. A passage leading to one of these magnificent buildings being open, I endeavoured with my
whole strength to move the machine towards it, and
with great difficulty accomplished my task. I now
entered into a spacious apartment, the floor of which
was composed of diamonds, emeralds, pearls, topazes,
and rubies. A large amber table stood in the centre,
and several amber chairs were also in this splendid
room. Without delay I determined to secure some
of the treasures by which I was surrounded, but
being closely wedged in and strongly cemented by

time, I was unable to unfasten them. I saw also
many rings, carcanets, and chains, of all manner of
precious stones, hanging loosely on the jasper walls,
by strings made of rushes. I was about to take them
down, when, just as I had edged myself within six
inches of them, I was unfortunately drawn back
through your want of line! In returning, I met
many comely mermen and beautiful mermaids, who
appeared to be the inhabitants of this blissful realm.
They were descending towards the splendid apartment which I have described, and were much
affrighted at my appearance, taking me, doubtless,
for some monstrous and new-created species."

LEGEND OF THE BLACK DOG.

"Be thou a spirit of health, or goblin damn'd,

*   *   *   *   *

Be thy intents wicked or charitable,
Thou com'st in such a questionable shape,
That I will speak to thee."

SHAKESPEARE.

An apparition, called in the Manks language the
Moddey Doo, in the shape of a large black spaniel
with curled shaggy hair, used to haunt Peel Castle,
and has been frequently seen in every room, but particularly the guard-chamber, where, as soon as the
candles were lighted, it came and lay down before
the fire, in presence of the soldiers, who at length, by
being so much accustomed to the sight of it, lost great
part of the terror they were seized with at its first
appearance. They still, however, retained a certain
awe, as believing it was an evil spirit, which only
waited permission to do them hurt; and, for that
reason, forbore swearing and profane discourse while

in its company. But though they endured the shock
of such a guest when altogether in a body, none
cared to be left alone with it. It being the custom,
therefore, for one of the soldiers to lock the gates of
the castle at a certain hour, and carry the keys to the
captain, to whose apartment the way led through the
church, they agreed among themselves that whoever
was to succeed the ensuing night his fellow in this
errand, should accomyany him that went first, and by
this means no man would be exposed singly to danger;
for I forgot to mention that the *Moddey Doo* was always
seen to come out from that passage at the close of
day, and return to it again as soon as morning
dawned, which made the soldiers look on this place
as its peculiar residence. One night a fellow being
drunk, and by the strength of the liquor rendered
more daring than ordinarily, laughed at the sim-
plicity of his companions; and although it was not
his turn to go with the keys, would needs take that
office upon himself to testify his courage. All the
soldiers endeavoured to dissuade him; but the more
they said, the more resolute he appeared, and swore
that he desired nothing more than that the *Moddey
Doo* would follow him as it had done the other
soldiers, for he would try whether it were dog or
devil. After having talked in a very reprobate
manner for some time, he snatched up the keys and
went out of the guard-room. In some time after
his departure a great noise was heard, but nobody
had the boldness to see what occasioned it, till, the
adventurer returning, they demanded the knowledge of him; but as loud and noisy as he had been
at leaving them, he was now become sober and silent
enough, for he was never heard to speak more; and
though all the time he lived—which was three days
—he was entreated to speak by all who came near
him, or if he could not do that to make some signs
by which they might understand what had happened

to him, yet nothing intelligible could be got from him; only that, by the distortions of his features and limbs, it might be guessed that he died in agonies more than is common in a natural death.

The *Moddey Doo*, however, was never after seen in Peel Castle, nor would any one attempt to go through that passage; for which reason it was closed up, and another was made. This accident happened about the year 1650.

THE BUGGANE OF ST. TRINION'S CHURCH.

" Ye who delight in old traditions,
    And love to talk of apparitions,
    Oh! listen, while I lay before ye
    My well-authenticated story."

This religious edifice is said to have been erected in fulfilment of a vow made by a person when in a hurricane at sea; but, according to tradition, it was never finished. This was attributed to the malice of a mischievous *Buggane*, or evil spirit, who, for want of better employment, amused himself with tossing the roof to the ground as often as it was on the eve of being finished, accompanying his achievement with a loud fiendish laugh of satisfaction. At length an attempt was made to counteract this singular propensity of the evil one. Tradition states that this attempt was made by Timothy, a tailor, of great pretentions to sanctity of character. On the occasion alluded to, the roof of St. Trinion's Church was, as usual, nearly finished, when the valorous tailor undertook to make a pair of breeches under it before the Buggane could commence his old trick. Accordingly, Timothy seated himself in the chancel, and began to work in great haste; but ere he had completed the breeches, the head of the frightful Buggane rose out of the ground before him, and addressed him thus:

"Do you see my great head, large eyes, and long teeth?"

"Hee! Hee!" (yes, yes,) replied Timothy, at the same time stitching with all his might, and not condescending to raise his eyes from his work.

The Buggane, still rising slowly out of the ground, cried in a more angry voice than before, "Do you see my great body, large hands, and long nails?"

"Hee! hee!" rejoined Timothy as before, but continuing to *pull out* with all his strength.

The Buggane, having now risen wholly from the ground, inquired in a terrific voice, "Do you see my great limbs, large feet, and long——?" But ere he could utter the last word, the valorous tailor put the finishing stitch into the breeches, and jumped out of the church just as the roof fell in with a crash. The fiendish laugh of the Buggane arose behind him as he bounded off in a flight, to which terror lent its utmost speed. Looking behind, he saw the frightful spectacle close upon his heels, with extended jaws, as if about to swallow him alive. To escape its fury, Timothy leaped into consecrated ground, where the Buggane had not power to follow; but, as if to punish him for his temerity, the malicious sprite lifted its great head from its shoulders, and threw it with great force to the feet of the tailor, where it exploded like a bomb-shell. Wonderful to relate, the adventurous Timothy was uninjured; but the church of St. Trinion remained without a roof.

FAIRY MINSTRELSY.

"Such a soft floating witchery of sound
As twilight elfins make, when they at eve
Voyage on gentle gales from fairy land."

CoLERIDGE.

An English gentleman, on his horse, was passing

over Douglas bridge before it was broken down; but the tide being very high, he was obliged to take the river, and did so without fear, as his horse was accustomed to swim. As he was in the middle of the river, he heard, or imagined he heard, such fine symphony that he thought nothing human ever came up to it. The horse was no less sensible of the harmony than himself, and notwithstanding the current of the tide, kept in an immovable posture all the time it lasted, which could not be less than three-quarters of an hour. He who before laughed at all the stories told of fairies, now became a convert.

MIRACLE IN THE ISLE IN MYRESCOGH.

"I say the tale as 'twas said to me."
SIR WALTER SCOTT.

There was a certain person called Donald, a veteran chieftain, and a particular favourite of Harald Olafson. This man, flying the persecution raised by Harald Gudrödson, took sanctuary with his infant child in St. Mary's Monastery, at Russin. Thither Harald Gudrödson followed, and, as he could not offer violence in this privileged place, he, in flattering and deceitful language, addressed the aged man to this purpose:—
"Why dost thou thus resolve to flee from me? I mean to do thee no harm." He then assured him of protection; adding, that he might depart in peace to any part of the country he had a mind. The veteran, relying on the solemn promise and veracity of the king, followed him out of the monastery. Within a short space, however, his Majesty manifested his sinister intentions, and demonstrated that he paid no regard to truth, or even his oath. He ordered the old man to be apprehended, bound, and carried to an isle

G

in the lake at Mirescog, where he was consigned over to the charge of a strong guard. In this distress, Donald still had confidence towards God. As often as he could conveniently bend his knees, he prayed the Lord to deliver him from his chains. The Divine interposition was not withheld. One day, as he was sitting in his chamber, and guarded only by two sentinels, suddenly the fetters dropped from his ankles, and left him at full liberty to escape. Concluding that this was wrought by the might of Heaven, he wrapped himself in his mantle, and taking to his heels, made the best of his way. One of the sentinels observing him, immediately started up and pursued. Having run a good way, eager to overtake the fugitive, he hit his shin a severe blow against a log; and thus, while posting at full speed, he was so arrested by the power of the Lord, that he could not stand. Hence, the good man, by the help of Heaven, got clear, and on the third day reached St. Mary's Abbey, at Russin, where he put up thanksgivings to God and the most merciful Mother for the deliverance. This declaration we have recorded from the man's own mouth.

THE PHYNNODDEREE.

> "Are you aught
> That man may question?"
> SHAKESPEARE.

Many stories are related by the Manks peasantry respecting the *phynnodderee*, a fallen fairy, who was banished from fairy-land for having paid his addresses to a pretty maid who lived in a bower beneath the blue tree of Glen Aldyn. He is doomed to remain in the Isle of Man till the end of time, transformed into a wild Satyr-like figure, covered with long shaggy hair, and was thence called the *phynnodderee*, or hairy one. The *phynnodderee* sometimes occupied himself in cutting down and gathering in meadow-grass, which would have been injured if allowed to remain exposed to the coming storm. On one occasion, a farmer having expressed his displeasure with the spirit for not having cut his grass close enough to the ground, the hairy one in the following year allowed the dissatisfied farmer to cut it down himself, but went after him stubbing up the roots so fast, that it was with difficulty the farmer escaped having his legs cut off by the angry sprite. For several years afterwards, no person could be found to mow the meadow, until a fearless soldier from one of the garrisons at length undertook the task. He commenced in the centre of the field, and by cutting round as if on the edge of a circle, keeping one eye on the progress of the scythe, while the other

> Was turned round with prudent care,
> Lest Phynnodderee catched him unaware,

he succeeded in finishing his task unmolested. This field, situate in the parish of Marown, hard by the ruins of the old church of St. Trinion's, is, from the circumstance just related, still called *yn cheance rhunt*, or the round meadow.

The following is one of the many stories related by the peasantry as indicative of the prodigious strength of the *phynnodderee*. A gentleman having resolved to build a large house and offices on his property, a little above the base of Sneafield mountain, at a place called *Sholt-e-will*, caused the requisite quantity of stones to be quarried on the beach, but one immense block of white stone, which he was very desirous to have for a particular part of the intended building, could not be moved from the spot, resisting the united strength of all the men in the parish. To the utter astonishment, however, of all, not only this rock, but likewise the whole of the quarried stones, consisting of more than an hundred cart-loads, were in one night conveyed

G 2

from the shore to the site of the intended house by the indefatigable *phynnodderee*, and in confirmation of this wonderful feat, the *white stone* is yet pointed out to the curious visitor.

THE WITCH.

"They say
Lamenting 's heard i' the air; strange screams of death."
SHAKESPEARE.

About two miles from Peel, opposite to the Tynwald Mount, there is a hill called Slieau Whuallin, said to be haunted by the spirit of a murdered witch; which, however, does not appear to mortal eyes, but every night joins its lamentations to the howling winds. This woman is said to have shared the fate of Regulus, having been put into a barrel with sharp iron spikes inserted round the interior, pointing inwards, and thus, by the weight of herself and the apparatus, allowed to roll from the top of the hill to the bottom.

A FAIRY TALE.

" 'Twas near an old enchanted court,
Where sportive faires made resort,
To revel out the night."
PARNELL.

A Manks man who had been led by invisible musicians for several miles together (not being able to resist the harmony), followed it till it conducted him to a large common, where were a great number of little people sitting round a table, eating and drinking in a very jovial manner. Among them were some faces whom he thought he had formerly seen, but forbore taking any notice, or they of him, till, the little people, offering him drink, one of them, whose features seemed not unknown to him, plucked him by the coat, and forbade him, whatever he did, to taste anything he saw before him; "for, if you do," added he, "you will be as I am, and return no more to your family." The poor man was much affrighted, but resolved to obey the injunction; accordingly, a large silver cup, filled with some sort of liquor, being put into his hand, he found an opportunity to throw what it contained on the ground. Soon after, the music ceasing, all the company disappeared, leaving the cup in his hand; and he returned home, though much wearied and fatigued. He went the next day and communicated to the minister of the parish all that had happened, and asked his advice how he should dispose of the cup; to which the parson replied, he could not do better than devote it to the service of the church; and this very cup, they say, is that which is now used for the consecrated wine in Kirk Malew.

THE SPELL-BOUND GIANTS.

"I'll read you matter deep and dangerous,
As full of peril and adventurous spirit
As to o'erwalk a current roaring loud,
On the unsteadfast footing of a spear."
SHAKESPEARE.

There is an apartment in Rushen Castle that has never been opened in the memory of man. The persons belonging to the Castle are very cautious in giving any reason for it; but the natives unconnected with the Castle assign this, *that there is something of enchantment in it.* They tell you that the Castle was at first inhabited by fairies, and afterwards by giants, who continued in possession of it till the days of

Merlin, who, by the force of magic, dislodged the greatest part of them, and bound the rest of them in spells, indissoluble to the end of the world. In proof of this, they relate a very strange story. They say there are a great many fine apartments under ground, exceeding in magnificence any of the upper rooms. Several persons of more than ordinary courage have in former times ventured down to explore the secrets of this subterranean dwelling-place, but none of them ever returned to give an account of what they saw. It was therefore judged expedient that all the passages to it should be continually shut, that no more might suffer by their temerity. About fifty-five years since, a person, possessed of uncommon boldness and resolution, begged permission to visit these dark abodes. Having obtained his request, he went down, and after some time returned, by the help of a clue of pack-thread which he took with him, and brought this amazing discovery: "That, having passed through a great number of vaults, he came into a long narrow place, which the further he penetrated he perceived that he went more and more on a descent. Having travelled for the space of a mile, he began to see a gleam of light, which, though it seemed to come from a vast distance, was the most delightful object he ever beheld. After having arrived at the end of that lane of darkness, he perceived a magnificent mansion, illuminated with many candles, whence proceeded the light which he had seen. Having, before he began the expedition, well fortified himself with brandy, he had courage enough to knock at the door of the mansion, which on the third knock was opened by a servant, who asked him what he wanted. 'I wish to go as far as I can,' replied our adventurer; 'be so kind as to direct me how to accomplish my design, for I see no passage but that dark cavern through which I came.' The servant informed him that he must pass through that mansion, and accordingly led

him through a long entry, and out at a back door.
He then walked a considerable distance, till he beheld another mansion more magnificent than that
through which he had recently passed; and, all the
windows being open, he observed innumerable lamps
burning in every room. Here also he designed to
knock, but had the curiosity to step on a little bank
which commanded a view of a low parlour, and looking in, he beheld a vast table in the middle of the
room, and on it, extended at full length, a monster at
least fourteen feet long, and about twelve round the
body. This prodigious fabric lay as if sleeping, with
a sword by his side, answerable to the hand of the
sleeping monster. This sight was more terrifying to
our adventurer than anything which he had ever
seen. He at once, therefore, resolved not to attempt
to enter into a place inhabited by persons of such a
monstrous stature, and returned in great haste to the
other mansion. The same servant appeared, and invited our traveller into the mansion; and, on learning
that he had gone as far as the abode of the monster,
informed him that if he had knocked at the door, he
would have seen company enough, but could never
have returned; on which our adventurer desired to
know what place it was and by whom possessed. The
servant replied, that these things were not be re-
vealed. The traveller then took his leave, and returned
by the same dark passage into the vaults; and shortly
afterwards ascended to the light of the sun."

THE GIANT'S CAVE.

"Come not between the dragon and his wrath!"
SHAKESPEARE.

At the foot of the mountain called Barrule, a giant's
cave may be seen. In this cave, it is believed that a

great prince, who never knew death, has been bound
by enchantment for the last six hundred years. A
huge dragon, with a tail and wings that darkened all
the elements, and eyes like two globes of fire, has
frequently been seen descending into this cavern, and
afterwards the most terrible shrieks and groans have
been heard. If a horse or dog is taken to the mouth
of the pit, its hair will stand on end, its eyes stare,
and a damp sweat will cover its whole body.

THE MAGICIAN'S PALACE.

"In visionary glory rear'd,
The gorgeous castle disappear'd;
And a bare heath's unfruitful plain,
Usurp'd the wizard's proud domain."

WARTON.

In the days of enchantment, a celebrated magician
erected, in the Isle of Man, the most magnificent palace
ever beheld, but it was solely inhabited by infernal
spirits. Every mortal who happened to venture within
its portals, was instantly converted into stone. This
spread such terror, that the country for many miles
round became desolate. One evening after dusk, it
happened that a poor man, looking for charity, was
travelling on that side of the island. He had never
heard of the enchanter. Seeing no place where he
might obtain lodgings for the night, he wandered
about a considerable time, until at length he came in
sight of the palace, which rose before him in all its
splendour; but, not presuming to enter within its
doors, lest he should be turned out again by some
churlish lacquey, he sat down under one of the large
piazzas by which the magnificent edifice was surrounded. Being hungry, he took some bread and

meat, with a little salt, out of his pocket, to eat; but a small portion of the salt having accidentally fallen to the ground, instantly terrific groans issued from the earth, a dreadful hurricane arose, lightning flashed around, and thunder rattled over his head. The gorgeous palace with its lofty porticoes and brazen door vanished, and the mendicant found himself in the midst of a barren waste. When he communicated this wonderful adventure to the inhabitants of the neighbouring village, they refused to believe him; till, having gone to the spot where the palace of the necromancer stood, they were convinced of the truth of the beggar's statement, and all united in prayers and thanksgivings for so great a deliverance. It appeared evident from the mendicant's story, that the salt which had been spilt upon the ground had occasioned the dissolution of the enchanter's palace. For this reason, salt has since been held in such high estimation with the Manks, that no person will go out to transact business without taking some in his pocket. Many will neither put out a child, nor take in one to nurse, without salt being mutually exchanged. Should any person ask the meaning of this veneration for salt, he will be told the above story, by doubting which he will incur the censure of the inhabitants of the island as a very profane individual.

THE APPARITION.

"He had not travelled so far in philosophy as to doubt the reality of witchcraft of apparitions."—SIR WALTER SCOTT.

A mighty bustle they make of an apparition, which they say haunts Castle Rushen, in the form of a woman who was executed some years ago for the murder of her child. I have heard not only persons who have been confined in the castle for debt, but also the soldiers of the garrison, affirm in the most positive manner that they have seen it at various times; but what I took most notice of was the report of a gentleman of whose good understanding as well as veracity I have a very great opinion. He told me, that happening to be abroad late one night, and caught in an excessive storm of wind and rain, he saw a woman standing before the castle gate, where, being not the least shelter, it something surprised him that anybody, much less one of that sex, should not rather run to some little porch or shed, of which there are several in Castletown, than choose to stand still, exposed and alone to such a dreadful tempest. His curiosity excited him to draw nearer to her, that he might discover who it was that seemed so little to regard the fury of the elements; but as he proceeded she retreated, and at last he thought she went into the castle, though the gates were shut. This obliging him to think he had seen a spirit, he went home very much terrified; but next day, on relating his adventure to some persons who lived in the castle, and describing as near as he could the garb and stature of the apparition, they told him it was that of the woman above mentioned, who had been frequently seen by the soldiers on guard to pass in and out of the gates of the castle, though they were locked and bolted, as well as to walk through the rooms, though there was no visible way of entering. But though she is so familiar to the eye of the inmates of the castle, no person has yet, however, had the courage to speak to her; and as they say a spirit has no power to reveal its mind without being conjured to do so in a proper manner, the reason of her being permitted to wander is unknown.

TEHI, THE ENCHANTRESS.

"She was a charmer."

SHAKESPEARE.

An enchantress, it is said, sojourned for a time in the Isle of Man. By her alluring arts, she ensnared the hearts of so many men around where she resided, causing them to neglect their occupations, that the country presented a scene of utter desolation. They neither ploughed nor sowed; the gardens were all overgrown with weeds; the once fertile fields were covered with stones; the cattle died for want of pasture; and the turf lay undug in the commons. This universal charmer, having brought things to such a deplorable crisis, under pretence of making a journey to a distant part of the Island, set out on a milk-white palfrey, accompanied by her numerous admirers on foot, till, having led them into a deep river, six hundred of them were drowned. She then flew away from the Isle of Man in the shape of a bat.

THE STORY OF THE MERMAID.

"The belief in mermaids, so fanciful and pleasing in itself, is ever and anon refreshed by a strange tale from the remote shores of some solitary islet."—SIR WALTER SCOTT.

During the time that Oliver Cromwell usurped the Government of England, few ships resorted to this island, which gave the mermen and mermaids frequent opportunities of visiting the shore, where, on moonlight nights they may be seen combing their hair; but as soon as they saw any one coming near them, they jumped into the water and were soon out of sight. Some persons who lived near the shore spread nets, and watched at a convenient distance for their approach ; but only one was taken, which proved to be a female. Nothing could be more lovely ; above the waist it resembled a fine young woman, but below that all was fish with fins and a spreading tail. She was carried to a house and used very tenderly ; but although they set before her the best provisions, she could not be prevailed upon to eat or drink, neither could they get a word from her, although they knew these creatures had the gift of speech. They kept her in the house three days, but perceiving that she began to look very ill by fasting so long, and fearing some great calamity would befal the island if they kept her till she died, they opened the door; on perceiving which, she raised herself on her tail from the place where she was lying, and glided with incredible swiftness to the sea-side. Her keeper followed at a distance, and saw her plunge into the water, where she was met by a great number of her own species, one of whom asked her what she had observed among the people on the earth. "Nothing," replied she ; "but they are so ignorant as to throw away the very water they have boiled their eggs in."

THE FAIRIES.

"Mona, once hid from those who search the main,
Where thousand elfin shapes abide."
COLLINS.

Some hundred years before the coming of our Saviour, the Isle of Man was inhabited, it is said, by fairies, and everything was carried on in a supernatural manner. A blue mist hung continually over

the island, preventing the ships that passed by from
having any suspicion that there was an island. This
blue mist was preserved by keeping a perpetual fire,
which, happening once by accident to be extinguished,
the shore discovered itself to several fishermen who
were then in a small boat on their vocation. Notice
was given to the people of a neighbouring country
by the fishermen; and the inhabitants of that country
at once despatched ships in order to make a further
discovery. When the men from the ships landed on
the island, they had a fierce encounter with the
fairies, and, having defeated them, took possession
of Rushen Castle, and shortly afterwards of the whole
island. The new conquerors maintained their ground
for a long time; but at length they were defeated by
a race of giants; and afterwards the giants were extirpated by Merlin, the famous British enchanter, in
the reign of Prince Arthur. The Isle of Man afterwards became the asylum of all the distressed princes
and great men in Europe; and for their better
security, it is asserted, the fortifications about Peel
Castle were made.

ST. MAUGHOLD AND GIL COLUM.

"Thenne of Maughold the Saynte thys story is,
    Of wycked Gil Colum lykewyse;
  A wonderous tale, yett so trewe ytt is,
    That noe bodye ytt denyes."

While Sumerlid was at Ramsey, in Man, in 1158,
he was informed that his troops intended to plunder
the Church of St. Maughold, where a great deal of
money had been deposited, in hopes that the veneration due to St. Maughold, added to the sanctity of

the place, would secure everything within its pre-cincts. One Gil Colum, a powerful chieftain, in par-ticular, suggested some very broad hints to Sumerlid about the money; and, besides, observed that he did not see how it was any breach of the peace against St. Maughold, if for the sustenance of the army, they drove off the cattle which were feeding round the churchyard. Sumerlid objected to this proposal, and said he would allow no violence to be offered to St. Maughold. Sumerlid at last, however, consented, though reluctantly, and pronounced these words: "Let the affair rest between thee, Gil Colum, and St. Maughold; let me and my troops be innocent; we claim no share of thy sacrilegious booty." Gil Colum, exceedingly happy at this declaration, ran back and ordered his vassals to assemble. He then desired that his three sons should be ready at daybreak to surprise the Church of St. Maughold, about two miles distant. That night, however, St. Maughold appeared to him as he lay asleep in his tent. The saint was arrayed in white, and had a pastoral staff in his hand. With this staff he struck Gil Colum to the heart three times. Awaking in great terror, he sent for the priests and clerks to make intercession for him, with the view, if possible, of obtaining the saint's forgiveness. The priests and clerks came. One of them pronounced the following imprecation: "May St. Maughold, who first laid his vengeful hand on thee, never remove thy plagues till he has bruised thee to pieces. Thus shall others, by seeing and hearing thy punition, learn to pay due respect to hal-lowed ground." The clergy then retired, and imme-diately such a swarm of monstrous filthy flies came buzzing about the ruffian's face and mouth, that neither he himself, nor his attendants, could drive them away. At last, about six o'clock in the morning, he expired in great misery and dismal torture. The exit of this man struck Sumerlid and his whole host with such dismay, that, as soon as the tide floated their ships, they weighed anchor, and with precipitancy returned home.

THE MERMAID'S REVENGE.

"I sat upon a promontory,
And heard a mermaid, on a dolphin's back,
Uttering such dulcet and harmonious breath,
That the rude sea grew civil at her song;
And certain stars shot madly from their spheres
To hear the sea-maid's music."

SHAKESPEARE.

There is a tradition in the Isle of Man, that a mermaid became enamoured of a young man of extraordinary beauty, took an opportunity of meeting him one day as he walked on the shore, and opened her passion to him, but was received with a coldness, occasioned by his horror and surprise at her appearance. This, however, was so misconstrued by the sea lady that, in revenge for his treatment of her, she punished the whole island by covering it with a mist; so that all who attempted to carry on any commerce with it, either never arrived at it, but wandered up and down the sea, or were on a sudden wrecked upon its cliffs.

LEGEND OF OLAF AND THE SWORD MACABUIN.

"All's well that ends well."

In the days of Olaf Gudrödson, there resided in Man a great Norman baron, named Kitter, who was so fond of the chase that he extirpated all the bisons and elks with which the island abounded at the time

of his arrival, to the utter dismay of the people, who,
dreading that he might likewise deprive them of their
cattle, and even of their purrs in the mountains, had
recourse to witchcraft to prevent such a disaster.
When this Nimrod of the north had destroyed all the
wild animals of the chase in Man, he one day extended
his havoc to the red deer of the Calf, leaving at his
castle, on the brow of Barrule, only the cook, whose
name was Eaoch (which signifies a person who can
cry loud), to dress the provisions intended for his
dinner. Eaoch happened to fall asleep at his work ;
the famous witchwife, Ada, caused the fat, accumu-
lated at the lee side of the boiling pot, to bubble over
into the fire, which set the house in a blaze. The as-
tonished cook immediately exerted his characteristic
powers to such an extent that he alarmed the hunters
in the Calf, a distance of nearly ten miles. Kitter,
hearing the cries of his cook, and seeing his castle in
flames, made to the beach with all possible speed, and
embarked in a small currach for Man, accompanied
by nearly all his attendants. When about half-way,
the frail bark struck on a rock (which from that circumstance has since been called Kitterland), and all
on board perished. The fate of the great baron and
the destruction, caused the surviving Norwegians to
believe that Eaoch, the cook, was in league with the
witches of the island to extirpate the Norwegians
then in Man, and on this charge he was brought to
trial and sentenced to suffer death. The unfortunate
cook heard his doom pronounced with great com-
posure, but claimed the privilege, at that time allowed
to criminals in Norway, of choosing the place and
manner of passing from time into eternity. This
was readily granted by the king. "Then," said the
cook with a loud voice, "I wish my head to be laid
across one of your majesty's legs, and there cut off
by your majesty's sword Macabuin, which was made
by Loan Maclibhuin, the dark smith of Drontheim."

It being known that the king's scimitar could sever even a mountain of granite, if brought into immediate contact with its edge, it was the wish of every one present that he would not comply with the subtle artifice of such a low varlet as Eaoch the cook; but his majesty would not retract the permission so recently given, and therefore gave orders that the execution should take place in the manner desired. Although the unflinching integrity of Olaf was admired by his subjects, they sympathized deeply for the personal injury to which he exposed himself, rather than deviate from the path of rectitude. But Ada, the witch, was at hand; she ordered toad's skins, twigs of the rowan tree, and adders' eggs, each to the number of nine times nine, to be placed between the king's leg and the cook's head, to which he assented. All these things being properly adjusted, the great sword Macabuin, made by Loan Maclibhuin, the dark smith of Drontheim, was lifted with the greatest caution by one of the king's most trusty servants, and laid gently on the neck of the cook. But ere its downward course could be stayed, it severed the head from the body of Eaoch, and cut all the preventatives asunder, except the last, thereby saving the king's leg from harm. When the dark smith of Drontheim heard of the stratagem submitted to by Olaf to thwart the efficacy of the sword Macabuin, he was so highly offended that he despatched his hammerman, Hiallus-nan-urd, who had only one leg, having lost the other when assisting in making that great sword, to the castle of Peel, to challenge King Olaf or any of his people to walk with him to Drontheim. It was accounted very dishonourable in those days to refuse a challenge, particularly if connected with a point of honour. Olaf, in mere compliance with this rule, accepted the challenge, and set out to walk against the one-legged traveller, from the

Isle of Man to the smithy of Loan Maclibhuin, in Drontheim.

They walked o'er the land and sailed o'er the sea;

and so equal was the match, that when within sight of the smithy, Hiallus-nan-urd, who was first, called to Loan Maclibhuin to open the door, and Olaf called out to shut it. At that instant, pushing past him of the one leg, the king entered the smithy first, to the evident discomfiture of the swarthy smith and his assistant. To show that he was not in the least fatigued, Olaf lifted a large fore-hammer, and under pretence of assisting the smith, struck the anvil with such force, that he clove it not only from top to bottom, but also the block upon which it rested. Emergaid, the daughter of Loan, seeing Olaf perform such manly prowess, fell so deeply in love with him, that during the time her father was replacing the block and the anvil, she found an opportunity of informing him that her father was only replacing the studdy to finish a sword that he was making, and that he had decoyed him to that place for the purpose of destruction, as it had been prophesied that the sword would be tem- pered in royal blood, and in revenge for the affront of the cook's death by the sword of Macabuin. "Is not your father the seventh son of *old Windy Cap*, King of Norway?" said Olaf. "He is," replied Emergaid, as her father entered the smithy. "Then," cried the King of Man, as he drew the red steel from the fire, "the prophecy must be fulfilled." Emergaid was unable to stay his uplifted hand, till he quenched the sword in the blood of her father, and afterwards pierced the heart of the one-legged hammerman, who, he knew, was in the plot for taking his life. This tragical event was followed by one of a more agree- able nature. Olaf, conscious that had it not been for the timely intervention of Emergaid, the sword of her father would indeed have been tempered in his blood, and knowing the irreparable loss which she had sustained at his hands, made her his queen, and from her were descended all succeeding kings of Man down to Magnus, the last of the race of Gudröd Crovan, the Conqueror.

THE MERMAID'S COURTSHIP.

"Come to our rich and starry caves,
Our home amid the ocean waves;
Our coral caves are walled around
With richest gems in ocean found,
And crystal mirrors, clear and bright,
Reflecting all in magic light."

A beautiful mermaid fell desperately in love with a young man who used to tend his sheep upon the rocks, and would often come on shore and sit down by his side, and present fine pearls, pieces of coral, and rare shells to him. These presents were invariably accompanied with smiles, pattings on the cheek, and all the marks of the most tender passion. One evening, it is said, she threw her arms eagerly around him; and the young man, imagining that she wished to draw him into the sea, struggled violently until he disengaged himself, and then scampered off as rapidly as he could. The mermaid, deeply affronted at this behaviour, seized a stone and threw it at him, and immediately glided into the sea. She was never afterwards seen on the island. The poor young man, though but slightly hit with the stone, felt from that moment such an acute pain that he cried continually for seven days, at the end of which he expired.

THE STORY OF IVAR AND MATILDA.

"The course of true love never did run smooth."

SHAKESPEARE.

There was a young and gallant knight, named
Ivar, who was enamoured of a very beautiful maiden,
named Matilda. He loved her ardently, and she
reciprocated his affection. From childhood they had
been companions, and as they grew up into years, the
firmer became they attached to each other. Never,
indeed were two beings more indissolubly bound by
the fetters of love than Ivar and Matilda. But
storms will overcast the serenest sky. At this period
Ragnvald was king of the Isle of Man; and, according to ancient custom, it was incumbent upon Ivar to
present his betrothed at the court of the monarch,
and obtain his consent, prior to becoming linked in
more indissoluble fetters with her. The nuptial day
had already been fixed, the feast had been prepared,
and it was noised abroad that the great and noble of
the island were to be present at the celebration of the
marriage. King Ragnvald resided in Rushen Castle,
in all the barbaric pomp which was predominant in
those olden times; and thither Ivar, accompanied by
Matilda, proceeded to wait upon him. Dismounting
from their horses at the entrance of the keep, they
were conducted to the presence of the king. Ivar
doffed his jewelled cap, and made obeisance; then
leading forward Matilda, he presented her to him.
Ragnvald was greatly enraptured with the maiden's
beauty from the first moment she had met his gaze,
and swore inwardly that he would possess her for
himself, and spoil the knight of his affianced bride.
To carry into effect his wicked purpose, he accused
Ivar of pretended crimes; and, ordering in his guards,
banished him from his presence, detaining, however,
the maiden. Vain would it be to attempt to depict

Matilda's anguish at this barbarous treatment. Ragnvald endeavoured to soothe her agitation, but it was to no purpose. He talked to her of his devoted love, but the maiden spurned his impious offers with contempt. Exasperated at her resistance, he had her confined in one of the most solitary apartments in the castle.

In the meantime, Ivar exerted himself to avenge the deep injury which he had received; but Ragnvald had such despotic sway, that all his endeavours proved abortive. At length he resolved to retire from the world, to assume the monastic habit, and to join the pious brotherhood of the monastery of St. Mary's, of Rushen. The brethren received him with joy, commiserating the bereavement which he had sustained. Ivar was now devoted to acts of piety; but still he did not forget his Matilda. Sometimes he would ascend the hill, and gaze towards the castle, wondering if Matilda were yet alive. One day, matin prayers having been offered up, Ivar wandered as usual through the woods, thinking of his betrothed, and bowed down with sorrow. At last he reclined on the grass to rest; when, looking around, he beheld a fissure in a rock which abutted from an eminence immediately opposite. Curiosity induced him to go near; and he discovered that it was the entrance to a subterranean passage. Venturing in, he proceeded for some distance. Onward he went, till a grated door arrested his progress. After some difficulty it yielded to his endeavours, and he passed through. Suddenly a piercing shriek, which reverberated along the echoing vaults, fixed him horror-struck for a moment to the place. It was repeated faintly several times. A faint glimmering of light now broke in upon his path, and he found himself in a vaulted chamber. Passing through it, another cry met his ear; and, rushing impetuously forward, he heard a voice in a state of exhaustion exclaim, "Mother of God, save

Matilda !" whilst, through a chink in the barrier, he beheld his long-lost love, with dishevelled hair and throbbing bosom, in the arms of the tyrant Ragnvald. Ivar instantly sprang through the barrier, rushed upon the wretch, and, seizing his sword, which lay carelessly on the table, plunged it into Ragnvald's bosom. Ivar, carrying Matilda in his arms, continued on through the subterranean passage, which brought them to the seaside, where they met with a boat which conveyed them to Ireland. There they were united in holy matrimony, and passed the remainder of their days in the raptures of a generous love, heightened by mutual admiration and gratitude.

THE END.

INDEX.

9 781343 254155